Coloring Outside the Lines:

Beyond the Break, Reclaiming My Story One Shade at a Time

DR. B.T. MCGUIRE

Copyright Page

Coloring Outside the Lines: Beyond the Break, Reclaiming My Story, One Shade at a Time
© 2025 by **Dr. B.T. McGuire**

All rights reserved. No part of this book may be reproduced, stored in a retrieval system, or transmitted in any form or by any means—electronic, mechanical, photocopying, recording, or otherwise—without prior written permission from the publisher, except for brief quotations in reviews or articles.

Published by **Dr. B.T. McGuire**
Nashville, TN

Hardcover ISBN: [**979-8-9927374-0-0**]
Paperback ISBN: [**979-8-9927374-1-7**]
eBook ISBN: [**979-8-9927374-2-4**]

Printed in the United States of America

For inquiries, permissions, or bulk purchases, contact:

Email: info@drbtmcguire.com
Website: www.drbtmcguire.com

This is a work of nonfiction. Some names and identifying details have been changed to protect the privacy of individuals. The views expressed are those of the author and do not necessarily reflect the views of any organizations or individuals mentioned.

For the kid who never stayed inside the lines, who was told to sit still, speak less, and follow the rules. This is your permission slip to take up space, to create in your own way, and to know that your story—messy, vibrant, and uncontained—is worth telling.

Author's Note

There was a time when I thought my story had to fit inside the lines drawn by others. That my voice had to be quieter. My presence had to be smaller. My dreams had to be more realistic. But life has a way of showing us that the most powerful stories aren't the ones neatly contained within the lines—they are the ones that spill beyond them, stretching past expectations, breaking through limitations, and filling spaces that were never meant to confine us in the first place.

Coloring Outside the Lines: *Beyond the Break, Reclaiming My Story, One Shade at a Time* is not just a memoir—it is a declaration. A love letter to resilience. A testament to the beauty of imperfection. It is about embracing every shade of who we are, even the ones we were once told to hide. It is about refusing to be discarded when the world suggests we are no longer useful. It is about coloring beyond the breaks, beyond the expectations, beyond the boundaries placed before us.

This book is for the ones who have been told they are too much. For the ones who have been made to believe they must shrink themselves to fit inside a world that was never meant to hold them back. For those who have questioned their worth, doubted their voice, or struggled to reclaim their space.

You don't have to stay within the lines someone else has drawn for you. You don't have to limit yourself to the shades the world assigns you. You are allowed to take up space. You are allowed to make mistakes. You are allowed to redefine the picture entirely.

Your story—messy, vibrant, uncontained—is yours to tell. And I hope this book gives you permission to tell it boldly.

—Dr. B.T. McGuire

Introduction:
The Colors of My Life

Renowned author and lecturer Allen Klein once said:

> *"Your attitude is like a box of crayons that color your world. Constantly color your picture gray, and your picture will always be bleak."*

Colors have a way of speaking without words. When we look at a painting, one of the first things that draws us in is the variety of colors—how they intimately call attention to a bigger picture. Color has the power to bring something to life.

Beyond art, color shapes our emotions, our memories, and the way we see the world. Imagine a life without color—how dull, how empty it would be. I often look at the greenness of the grass, the different shades of blue in the sky, the fire-red glow of a sunset, and I know that no part of this world was meant to exist in monotony. Each color tells a story. Each shade carries a meaning.

Colors evoke emotions—some warm, some cool, some comforting, some unsettling. Take orange, for example: while it is a warm color, it conveys happiness, upliftment, and positivity. Colors cause us to feel, as the young folks say, *some type of way*.

But you don't have to take my word for it. Let's try an activity:

1. Close your eyes and think of your favorite color.
2. When you think of this color, how does it make you feel? Jot down those emotions.
3. Think of items that are your favorite color. What do you like about those items?
4. Now, open your eyes.

The first time I traveled to Europe, I was eager to immerse myself in the art, culture, and history I had only read about in books.

Paris, with its grandeur and elegance, was like a painting itself—every street filled with a blend of old and new, a city alive with color. But nothing compared to the moment I stepped into the Louvre Museum and saw the Mona Lisa up close.

I had seen pictures of da Vinci's famous work countless times, but standing there in the crowded gallery, looking at the painting itself, I noticed something different. The way the light and shadows played across her face, the depth of the colors—subtle yet deliberate. There was a mystery in her eyes, a quiet knowing. People from all over the world stood around me, trying to capture her expression through their phone screens, but I stood still, letting the moment soak in.

It struck me that colors in art are never random. Every shade, every stroke of the brush has meaning. The muted golds and soft browns of the Mona Lisa's portrait told a story of depth and complexity, much like life itself. And just like in life, we sometimes only see the full picture when we take a step back.

That visit to the Louvre reminded me that color isn't just something we see—it's something we experience. It shapes how we interpret the world, how we define beauty, how we remember the past, and how we create meaning in the present.

As I wandered deeper into the museum, I found myself in the African Art section. The rich, earthy tones of the masks, sculptures, and textiles told stories of civilizations that thrived long before the Louvre was ever built. The deep browns of wooden carvings, the bold reds and blacks in ceremonial masks, the intricate gold detailing on ancient artifacts—all these colors carried history, resilience, and culture. Each piece stood as a testament to the creativity and depth of African heritage, an undeniable imprint on global artistry.

Looking at these works, I was reminded that art—like identity—is not confined to one frame, one region, or one interpretation. The presence of African art in the same space as da Vinci's Mona Lisa reinforced something I had always known: Black culture, Black history, and Black artistry are just as significant, just as masterful, and just as enduring.

Yet as I took in the grandeur of these works, a quiet thought crept into my mind: Why were these treasures here and not in their countries of origin? It was a moment that reminded me of something much deeper—how often Black culture and contributions are celebrated, yet not always fully seen for what they are. It made me think about my own life, the moments where I felt I had to fight to be seen, to be acknowledged for my depth beyond the surface.

There was a time when I, too, felt like a forgotten piece of art, placed in a space where people admired me but didn't truly understand the history, struggle, and richness behind what they saw.

Color influences how we perceive the world, shaping our emotions, memories, and even the way we move through society. Psychologists have long studied how different colors affect mood—blue evokes calmness, red signals urgency, yellow promotes happiness. But beyond psychology, color also carries deep societal weight. In spaces where Black individuals exist, color often determines how we are perceived, how we are treated, and whether or not our presence is truly valued.

For centuries, society has associated black with mystery, power, elegance, and fear. And for Black individuals, that perception has shaped our lived experience. We exist in spaces where our voices are heard but not always valued. Like shadows, we are seen but sometimes intentionally overlooked. To be Black in America is to constantly fight to be recognized for the fullness of who we are—beyond stereotypes, beyond misconceptions, beyond the limits imposed on us.

Black individuals frequently navigate environments where they are visible yet unseen—acknowledged but not fully embraced. Whether in corporate spaces, academic institutions, or media portrayals, there is a delicate balancing act of being present while ensuring that presence is not deemed too loud, too bold, too disruptive. This experience mirrors the paradox of African art in the Louvre: admired, displayed, yet detached from its origin and stripped of full context. Just as these artifacts tell a rich history beyond what is captured in a museum exhibit, Black existence holds depth beyond surface-level recognition. But just like black absorbs all light, it also holds all possibilities. Black is strength, resilience, and boundless potential.

For Black Americans, color has always been more than just an aesthetic—it's a language, a form of resistance, and a declaration of existence in a world that often tried to erase us.

Think about the Pan-African colors—red, black, and green—each symbolizing the blood, the people, and the land. Think about the Civil Rights Movement, where activists dressed in bold suits, sharp colors, and Afros, showing that we could be both radical and regal. Think about how the Black church is filled with bright hats, vibrant choir robes, and rich gold crosses.

Color has always been a statement of identity, pride, and freedom. Even gospel music, a powerful force in the Black faith community, is full of references to color. From *Amazing Grace*, where we sing about being "blind but now I see," to spirituals that reference golden streets and bright heavens, color has always played a role in how we interpret faith and liberation.

And yet, for many Black children—myself included—the first thing the world tries to do is dim our colors. Historically, Black communities have reclaimed colors as an assertion of power. The vibrant shades of African textiles, the expressive nature of Black fashion, and even the colorful murals that adorn our neighborhoods serve as reminders that our history is rich, bold, and full of life.
Even in the midst of struggle, color is how we continue to define ourselves on our own terms.

I want to share a story with you that inspired the title of this book. As a first grader at Mary G. Hogsett Elementary in Danville, Kentucky, I often stood out. First grade is a pivotal year in a child's life, but for me, it was one of my first lessons in resilience. My homeroom teacher made me feel as though I was unfit to be in her class.

She described me as a disruption, claimed I couldn't keep up, and even requested that I be removed. She made me feel inadequate—not because of my abilities, but because she lacked the ability to see me.

The ability to truly see students is essential in education, and it goes far beyond test scores and behavior charts. It requires social-emotional learning and culturally relevant pedagogy, two frameworks that my teacher completely ignored. Social-emotional learning is an approach that helps students develop self-awareness, emotional regulation, and interpersonal skills. It recognizes that students don't just bring their brains into the classroom; they bring their hearts, their lived experiences, and their struggles. If my teacher had been trained in SEL, she would have recognized that I was a child seeking connection, not a disruption to be removed.

Culturally relevant pedagogy is about making education meaningful by affirming students' identities and valuing their cultural backgrounds. It challenges the idea that one type of knowledge, one way of being, is superior to others. Instead of seeing me as an energetic, curious Black boy, my teacher saw me as a problem. She did not see my culture, my history, or my potential—just my presence as something to be managed. To her, I was just another rowdy Black boy.

I remember the sting of her words, the way she spoke about me as if I were defective, something that needed fixing. I stopped raising my hand. I stopped speaking up. I began to believe that maybe she was right—maybe I wasn't smart enough, maybe I didn't belong.

One day, she sent me to the principal's office for what she deemed "extreme disruption." On my way there, I carried a Color by Number assignment in one hand and a brand-new box of crayons in the other. When I arrived, our school secretary greeted me warmly.

"Hi, Bryson! Have a seat and work on your coloring sheet. The principal will be with you shortly." I did as I was told, opening my crayon box and beginning to color. I reached for my blue crayon and, just as I started, it snapped in two. Frustrated, I huffed and looked down at the broken piece in my hand.

At first, I tried to use it anyway, but the jagged edge wouldn't glide smoothly like before. It wobbled in my grip, slipping across the page, streaking color beyond the carefully drawn lines of my assignment. I pressed harder, trying to force control, but instead, the blue sprawled in unexpected directions.

For a moment, I panicked—this wasn't how it was supposed to look. The lines were there for a reason, weren't they? But then, I noticed something different. The bold, uneven strokes gave the picture a new kind of depth. The color bled beyond the borders, making it feel more alive, more real.

It wasn't perfect, but it was mine. Still, frustration lingered. I huffed and stood up to throw the broken crayon away. "Is something bothering you, Bryson?" she asked. "My crayon broke," I muttered. "Now I can't use it."

She signaled for me to come to her desk. Taking the broken crayon, she carefully peeled back the excess paper, revealing the crayon's full surface again. Then, she picked up a blank sheet of paper and began to draw with it. Stripes of blue filled the page. I stared in shock.

"How are you able to use that?" I asked. "I thought my crayon was broken." She smiled. "Just because it's broken doesn't mean it doesn't work. Now, you have two blue crayons." That moment stayed with me. I had been ready to throw away something that still had purpose—something that could still color, still create, still leave a mark. I looked down at my own picture, now colored outside the lines, and realized something else. She placed the crayon back in my hand and said gently, "Remember, broken crayons still color."

That was the first time I realized that brokenness doesn't mean the end; sometimes, it's an opportunity to color in new ways. That day, I started to see myself differently. If a broken crayon could still be used, maybe I could still be valuable, too. Maybe I wasn't the problem. Maybe I wasn't meant to stay inside the lines that others had drawn for me. Maybe I was supposed to color beyond the breaks.

And isn't that just like life? We all have moments where we feel broken. We all have seasons where we feel discarded. But broken crayons still color.

Each of us is a unique shade, shaping a larger masterpiece. In this book, I invite you to explore my life as a spectrum of colors—each one revealing a part of my journey.

Black is my foundation—the power, resilience, and heritage that make me who I am.

Red is the fire that fuels—driven by passion, ignited by struggle, and sustained by the boldness to keep pushing forward, even when the cost is high.

Yellow is joy—the triumphs, the light, the moments worth celebrating.

Gray is doubt—the in-between moments, the uncertainties, the lessons learned in stillness.

Blue is healing—the moments of peace in self-worth.

Pink is compassion—the journey of self-love and embracing all that I am.

Green is growth—the evolution of who I am becoming.

White is faith—the guiding force that has kept me going.

Orange is creativity—how I've expressed myself in a world that often tried to silence me.

Purple is wisdom—the lessons I've learned along the way.

Brown is home—the foundation of family, tradition, and stability.

Gold is legacy—the mark I want to leave on the world.

Life is not just one color—it is a masterpiece painted with many. Each stroke, whether inside or outside the lines, tells a story of resilience, transformation, and self-discovery. Some colors are bold and unafraid, others are quiet but deeply meaningful. Some shades were once faded, but I have reclaimed them—one by one, piece by piece.

For so long, I believed my story had to fit within the lines drawn by others. But real beauty, real growth, comes when we dare to color beyond the breaks, beyond expectations, beyond what was once defined for us. This book is my journey—my way of reclaiming my story, one shade at a time.

Chapter 1: Black

The Roots That Shaped Me

Black is more than a color—it is a history, a lineage, a tapestry woven from the lives of those who came before me. It is the echo of my ancestors' voices, the weight of their sacrifices, and the foundation upon which I stand. Poet Theresa THA SONGBIRD once said: *"Black is not something we get to choose, but something we get to cherish."* I did not choose to be Black. But Black chose me. And what a gift it is.

My DNA tells a story that history books often overlook—a story of strength, survival, and resilience. According to my ancestry results, I am 49% Nigerian, with a direct lineage to the Yoruba people, one of the largest ethnic groups in West Africa. The Yoruba have a history deeply rooted in art, spirituality, and governance, tracing their origins to the Oyo and Ife Kingdoms, which flourished long before European colonization. Their civilization thrived on vast trade networks, intricate storytelling traditions, and a deeply spiritual worldview that connected them to the land and each other.

But history took a violent turn.

Like millions of Africans, my ancestors were forcibly taken from their homeland during the transatlantic slave trade. Many were transported to the American South, where they were enslaved on plantations, forced to labor in fields of cotton, tobacco, and hemp. The Yoruba people, known for their resilience, carried their culture with them—embedding it into the rhythms of Black American life through music, language, and spiritual practices. Despite their captivity, they found ways to hold onto their identity, passing down traditions that would shape future generations. Their journey from freedom to bondage, and from bondage to perseverance, is the foundation upon which my family's story is built.

Long before I was born, before my family planted its roots in Danville, Kentucky, my ancestors lived in Paris, Kentucky, in Bourbon County—a place where the land told stories of toil and survival.

My great-great-great-grandfather, Charles Bedinger (1840–unknown), was likely born into slavery, in a region known for its tobacco and hemp plantations—industries that thrived on the backs of enslaved Black men and women. He survived an America that saw him as property before he was able to claim his own name, his own family, and his own place in history.

He married Mary A. Harris (1850–unknown), and together they had nine children, including Anderson Bedinger (1872–1963), my great-great-grandfather. Anderson was the first in our family to be born free. For him, freedom was not just a birthright—it was a responsibility. As a young man, he left Bourbon County and migrated to Danville, Kentucky, in search of opportunity, carving out a life in a world that still sought to keep Black men in chains—if not physically, then economically and socially. He married Bertha S. Bedinger (1895–1966), and together, they raised a family in the heart of a segregated South.

One of their children, my great-grandfather, Calvin Bedinger (1910–1979), carried that same resilience forward. He married my great-grandmother, Malvena Barnes Bedinger (1915–2011), a strong Black woman who left behind a legacy of perseverance and faith. Their daughter, Sharon Lee Bedinger, my grandmother, would become one of the most influential figures in my life.

When I hear the word "hero," one person in particular comes to mind—my grandfather, Alonzo McGuire. Papa was raised by his mother in Louisville, Kentucky, but in 1957, at just 15 years old, my grandfather made a decision that would alter the course of our family's history—he left Louisville and moved to Danville. At an age when most teenagers were concerned with school and friendships, he was stepping into an entirely new world, one that was smaller in size but no less complicated. Louisville, a city with a rich Black culture and thriving communities, had offered him a certain anonymity, a sense of being part of something bigger. But in Danville, everything was smaller—more intimate, more scrutinized, more defined by racial lines that weren't just implied but enforced.

For a young Black boy in 1957, moving into a town like Danville was more than just a change in scenery—it was a shift in power dynamics, in opportunities, in what it meant to be seen and unseen. The weight of segregation was different in a smaller town, where the expectations of where you could go, who you could be, and what you could achieve were clear and largely unspoken. He wasn't just moving; he was entering a new chapter where his Blackness would be even more under a microscope.

But my grandfather was not a man to be limited. He took the values of hard work and resilience with him and built a life that would eventually command the respect of those around him. He didn't just survive Danville; he shaped it. He established himself as a force in the community, known for his strength, integrity, and work ethic. And in doing so, he carved out space not just for himself but for the generations that would follow.

His journey wasn't just about adapting to a new place—it was about defying the limitations that came with it. And in that defiance, he laid the foundation for a family legacy that would continue to grow, long after he first stepped onto Danville's soil as a 15-year-old boy with a future yet to be written. Papa was, is, a Danville legend, a household name.

My grandmother, on the other hand, was a native of Danville, with deep family roots in the city. The majority of my close family connections and relationships stem from her side of the family. Papa and Granny met at Bate High School in 1962 and later married in 1967. Bate High School was a pillar of Black excellence, named after John W. Bate, an educator who turned a one-room schoolhouse into a fully accredited high school for Black students.

Papa graduated from Bate High School and soon after joined the United States Army, pursuing a career in the Armed Forces. My grandmother, a member of Bate's final graduating class before integration, watched as the school transitioned into Bate Middle School in 1964. Shortly after, in 1967, my father was born.

As the oldest grandchild, I spent many summers with my grandparents. Being the only grandchild for six years, I had the privilege of forming a special bond with them. Their house was my safe haven, a place where I felt secure, loved, and protected. Like many older Black people, daytime television consisted of watching their "stories". The stories were what my grandparents called the soap operas. I can still recall their tv schedule during the summers as a child:

9AM: Victor Newman would be stirring up something on The Young and the Restless.

10AM: Judge Joe Mathis would be setting them straight on Court TV.

11AM: Plinko would be the game that everybody wanted to play with Bob Barker on The Price is Right.

12PM: This time slot was for Family Feud, depending on who was competing. If Granny didn't like the demographics of the contestants, she would watch Lex18 News at 12.

1PM: That Marlena was probably on her fifth death, and Bo and Hope were wearing us all thin on Days of Our Lives.

2PM: This was usually the time that we ran our errands. Granny always seemingly had something to do while Papa was at work.

3PM: After we got back from running errands, this was my time to watch tv. Sadly, there was no time left because my Dad got off of work at 3:30PM and at...

4PM: Daddy would be at their house to pick me up.

While I possess fond memories of my grandparents as a child, I can't tell my story without telling the story of my parents. Like my grandparents, my parents met within the Danville school system. Both graduates of Danville High School's Class of 1987, they are in every sense of the phrase "high school sweethearts." They have loved each other for over 40 years, marrying in September 1999.

My father is a manly man, yet his heart is full of gold. His philosophy was simple: "If I got it, you got it." That wasn't just about money—it was about love, guidance, and protection.

He worked in a local factory, ensuring that our family always had what we needed. He was the kind of man who led by example, who believed that hard work wasn't just a means to an end but a reflection of character. No matter how tired he was after a long shift, he showed up—whether it was helping with homework, grilling out on Sundays, or making sure the oil in my car was changed before I even thought to ask.

His hands, calloused from years of labor, built a life where we never had to question if we were cared for. While he said 'I love you' often, but he didn't have to—his love was in the way he worked, in the way he sacrificed, in the way he made sure that even when times were hard, we never felt the weight of it. That was his version of love: steadfast, unwavering, always present.

Perhaps one of my fondest memories of Daddy as a child was bedtime. Every night, Daddy would stop by each of our rooms to wish us goodnight and tell us that he loved us. After he got to my room, he would head straight to their room, get on his knees, and pray. I watched him do this until the day I moved out for college. This was one of the first examples of prayer that I remember— acts such as these would also shape who we are today. He never missed a night. Aside from his home life, Daddy played softball in a couple of local leagues within the city. I remember we would travel frequently for those Softball Tournaments during the summers.

To this day, when I think about the kind of man I strive to be, I think of my father—not just in his strength, but in his quiet, constant generosity. As an adult, there are many things that I sometimes question my father about. However, there is always one thing that I know to be true… My father loves my mother with all of his heart.

My mother, on the other hand, was the backbone of our family unit—a woman of prayer, grace, and strength. Mother has always been and continues to be a kind and gentle soul. Yet, we knew not to step out of line with her.

In every sense of the word, I am my mother's twin. My mother was 24 years old when I came into this world. While many consider 18 or 21 to be the magic numbers that an individual enters into adulthood, I could argue that my mother and I grew up together. As Daddy was frequently working or busy outside of the house and being an only child for eight years, the majority of my childhood was spent with her. I am truly my mother's child. If you have seen and experienced one, you have seen and experienced the other. Just as Jesus said, 'If you have seen me, you have seen the Father,' my mother and I are reflections of each other—her faith, her fire, her resilience all live within me.

She was the glue that held us together, ensuring that our home was not just a place of residence, but a sanctuary of love and stability. No matter what challenges arose, she met them with unwavering determination and faith. She balanced work, family, and the unspoken labor that so many Black women carry—raising strong children while navigating a world that often tried to overlook her strength.

One of my earliest memories of her was our morning routine before school. Before she even woke us up, she would take time for herself, preparing for the day ahead. This meant frequent prayers and making sure breakfast was ready before we ever opened our eyes. I can still hear her singing and praying in the shower before she came to wake us. After getting us up and ready for school, she would send us off on the bus before heading to work a full-time job.

By 5 PM, she was back home, cooking a full-course meal—always meat and at least two sides. We never ate leftovers; she cooked fresh meals daily, ensuring that dinner was not just about nourishment but about family. Every night, we sat down together to eat, no matter how busy life became. After dinner, she prepared us for bed, ironed our clothes for the next day, ironed her clothes, and ironed Daddy's clothes. Sometimes, she wouldn't get to bed until 11 PM, but not before she would sneak into our rooms, anoint us with oil and lay hands on us, only to wake up and do it all over again at 5 AM.

Every morning, she would burst into my room, flip on the light, and yell: "Rise and shine, give God the glory!" At the time, it *annoyed* me. But looking back, I know it was her way of covering me in prayer before I stepped into a world that wasn't always kind to Black boys with big dreams. There were times when I leaned on those prayers more than I ever realized. In moments of uncertainty, when doors closed or challenges seemed insurmountable, I could still hear her voice: *Rise and shine, give God the glory.* Whether it was preparing for exams, navigating professional setbacks, or finding the strength to advocate for myself in spaces that weren't built for me, her words stayed with me.

Faith has remained a guiding force in my life. It is the unwavering belief that there is purpose in the journey, even when the path isn't clear. My mother's prayers weren't just a morning ritual; they were a foundation, one that carried me through every obstacle I faced.

My mother was relentless in ensuring that my brother and I had every opportunity she never had. She often spoke about how she wished her own family had pushed her harder to pursue her dreams—how she had the potential for more but lacked the guidance and encouragement to reach for it. That realization shaped the way she raised us. She refused to let us settle for mediocrity. Every late night spent reviewing homework, every early morning wake-up call, every lesson in discipline and faith—it was all intentional. She was determined that we would never look back on our lives with regret, wondering what could have been. Her sacrifices weren't just about providing for us; they were about pushing us toward something greater. She instilled in us the belief that we could go further, dream bigger.

My parents taught us that sacrifice doesn't always look like suffering. Sometimes, it looks like staying up late to make sure your kids' clothes are pressed, even when your own mind is heavy with stress. Sometimes, it looks like showing up with a full-course meal at 5 PM, even though you worked eight hours on your feet. They never let us see any struggles. But looking back, I realize they were fighting battles every day—battles they never let touch us.

My younger brother, Brennen, is my pride and joy. Being a big brother has been one of the greatest joys of my life. From the moment Brennen was born, I knew that I had a responsibility—not just to protect him, but to guide him, to be a role model, to pave the way so he wouldn't have to navigate life's challenges alone. I took pride in teaching him things, whether it was how to tie his shoes or how to talk his way out of trouble when we both knew he was guilty.

There's a unique kind of joy that comes with being the older sibling—the privilege of watching someone grow, of knowing that your words, your actions, and your presence shape who they become. I remember the first time Brennen looked up to me, not just as his brother, but as someone he admired. It was in the small moments—the way he mimicked my phrases, tried to dress like me, or waited for my approval before making a decision. It was both humbling and an honor.

And just as my mother pushed us toward something greater, I carried that same responsibility for my brother. I wanted him to know that he could dream bigger, reach higher, and that I would always be there, just a step ahead, making sure he knew the path was clear.

As Brennen matured and graduated high school, he played college football, chasing the dream that so many young Black boys grow up with. But while the NFL didn't become his future, education did. Brennen went on to earn a master's degree in business, proving that success isn't about one path—it's about resilience, adaptability, and drive. Together, Brennen and I are first-generation college students.

From the plantations of Bourbon County to the classrooms of today, I have become the manifestation of my ancestors' wildest dreams. I am an educator—a former middle school teacher, principal, and now a college professor. In 2020, I earned my doctorate, breaking barriers Charles and Mary, Anderson and Bertha, and Calvin and Malvena could have never imagined.

The love that surrounded me was not ordinary—it was generational, it was protective, it was all-encompassing. My family's legacy was not just in their names, but in the sacrifices they made to ensure I could walk into rooms they had never been allowed to enter. My granddad, a legend in Danville, built a reputation on strength, on resilience, on the kind of work ethic that demanded respect. His presence was a blueprint—one that shaped how my father led, how my grandmother nurtured, how my mother sacrificed. And that love? It was not just warm; it was fierce. It was the kind of love that ensured I would never feel small, never feel unseen, never feel anything less than destined for greatness. It was a love that whispered, *"You will be more than we ever could be, and we will be here—always."*

Moving beyond the broad lens of racial difference, I want to take a moment to reflect on how these realizations first surfaced in my personal life. My family was my first home, my first understanding of the world, my first exposure to love and identity. Within our walls, I was safe. I was celebrated. I was whole. But the moment I stepped outside, the rules shifted.

I remember the first time I truly understood that I was Black—not just as a fact of my existence, but as something that shaped the way the world saw me.

It was the sixth grade. Being from a rural city, the pickings for dating were small, and usually white. I remember my first girlfriend. We were gearing up to go to the school dance—my first middle school dance. I asked the young lady to go with me, and she said yes. The next day, she came back to me, her face hesitant, her words slow and deliberate. She told me that she couldn't go with me anymore because her mother had forbidden it. "She said I couldn't date *niggers*."
I had never heard that word before, yet it stung.

I went home that evening and told my parents the story, unsure of why it hurt so much. My mother looked at me, sadness and something fiercer flashing in her eyes. She explained what it meant, how it had been used against our people for generations, how it was a word meant to wound and diminish. Then, she stood up, grabbed her keys, and knocked on that woman's door. Yeah, that wasn't a pretty sight.

I didn't sleep much that night. My mind replayed her words over and over, not because I understood them fully, but because I couldn't understand *why*. Why was this different? Why did her mother care? What did it mean for me?

The next morning, I walked into school feeling different. Up until that moment, I had thought of myself as just another kid—Bryson, the one who loved to laugh, who talked too much in class, who ran too fast on the playground. But that day, I wasn't just Bryson anymore. I was *Black Bryson*.

I soon realized that the word *"nigger"* didn't just mean rejection—it carried the weight of history, of suffering, of exclusion. That word made me question: was there something about me that was unacceptable? Was my very existence a problem? These moments were not just encounters with hate; they were initiations into the lifelong journey of understanding what it means to be Black in America.

Everything felt like it had shifted. I started noticing things I had overlooked before. The way some teachers expected me to be louder than I was. The way some of my white classmates assumed I liked rap music or played sports even though I had never told them that. The way I was always the one who got blamed first when a group got too rowdy in class.

At lunch, one of my friends—a white boy I had known since kindergarten—asked why I looked so serious. I hesitated before I told him what happened. His face turned red, and he mumbled something about how his mom *wouldn't care who he dated*. But then, as if to reassure himself, he said, "I mean, you're not like… other Black kids."

And there it was. I was always aware that I existed in the in-between. I was too "proper" for some, too "Black" for others. I didn't fit the mold of what people expected a Black boy to be. I wasn't an athlete. I wasn't a troublemaker. I wasn't someone who took up space in the ways they had assumed I should. And that difference followed me, sometimes making me feel like I had to prove myself, like I had to compensate for not being "Black enough" or not being relatable enough. It wasn't until later that I realized my Blackness was not something to conform—it was something to define on my own terms.

A large part of what made me different was the foundation I had at home. I grew up in a two-parent household, something that was often seen as an exception rather than the norm in the narratives people projected onto Black families. My parents provided stability, love, and expectations that pushed me to strive for excellence. There was never a question of whether I would go to college—it was understood. There was never a question of whether I would be respectful, responsible, and carry myself with dignity—those values were instilled in me from an early age.

But that foundation also set me apart. It made me hyperaware of the way people perceived me. Teachers, classmates, and even other Black kids sometimes made assumptions about who I was before I had the chance to show them. My family prioritized education and discipline, so I spoke a certain way, carried myself a certain way. Some people called it "acting white." Others assumed I was trying to be better than them. But the truth was, I was just being raised in an environment where expectations were high, and I had no other choice but to rise to them.

That was the day I learned that my Blackness wasn't just something I *was*—it was something the world had *expectations* about. Even at twelve years old, I knew what that meant. I had been categorized, measured, *judged*—and I had somehow made it past an imaginary line in his mind. I wasn't sure if I was supposed to be relieved… or insulted.

To exist in Black skin is to inherit a burden—one woven through generations of oppression, resistance, and survival. The weight of being Black is knowing that history lives in our blood, that the past is never far behind, and that the fight for dignity is never over.

It means living with the reality that our ancestors' struggles did not end with emancipation. That systemic barriers, economic disparities, and racial biases are not just relics of the past but persistent forces shaping our present. It means understanding that every opportunity we seize was once denied to those who came before us, and that our success is more than personal—it is collective.

It is knowing that the cost of freedom was paid in blood, sweat, and sacrifice. That our history is written in ink, but also in the crimson of those who marched, who fought, who bled, and who died so that we could walk a little taller. It is recognizing that while progress has been made, the battle is far from over.

To be Black in America is to carry both the blessing and the burden of our history. It is knowing that we are our ancestors' wildest dreams and yet, in many ways, still fighting the battles they started. We are proof of survival, but survival itself requires sacrifice.

Every opportunity I've had—the education, the freedom, the voice I now have—was paid for by the generations before me. By the blood spilled in cotton fields, by the marches on bridges, by the hands that built a country that did not love them back.

And through it all, I carry Blackness as my foundation. Black is foundational. Black is strength. Black is resilience.

Chapter 2: Red

The Fire That Fuels Me

They say fire can either destroy or refine. It can consume everything in its path, leaving nothing but ash—or it can forge something stronger, stripping away the unnecessary and leaving only what can withstand the heat.

For me, red represents the fire that fuels me. My ambition was not born out of mere desire—it was forged in the crucible of my K-12 educational experiences. Every lesson, every challenge, and every barrier I faced in school shaped the fire that propelled me forward.

From a young age, I understood that school was not just a place of learning—it was a battleground for identity, opportunity, and recognition. I saw the disparities in how students were treated, how expectations varied depending on who you were and where you came from. I learned quickly that excellence was my only option if I wanted to be seen, valued, and respected. I carried the unspoken understanding that I would have to work twice as hard, not just for myself, but for the generations before me who never had the same opportunities—but that fire has always come at a cost. Ambition, for Black men in America, is rarely just about drive or passion—it is about survival. It is about knowing that the world is not built to hand you success and that every inch of progress must be fought for, earned, and sometimes even taken.

Early on, I understood that ambition was not just encouraged in my household—it was demanded. I was raised to know that mediocrity was not an option. That lesson came from my mother, who drilled into me and my brother the reality of our existence: *"You are a Black man in America. That means you already have two strikes against you, and you will always have to work twice as hard to get half of what you deserve."*

When my mother first told me that I would have to work twice as hard to get half as much, it could have planted a seed of bitterness in me. It could have made me resent the reality that I would always be expected to overperform just to be seen as worthy. But instead, it prepared me. It hardened me in a way that wasn't about resentment, but about resilience. It wasn't about discouragement—it was about equipping me for a world that would not always be fair.

Growing up, I lived in two worlds: the one inside my home and the one outside of it. Inside, I was deeply loved, celebrated, and reminded of my potential. Outside, I was often met with doubt, low expectations, and systems designed to overlook me. My mother's words weren't meant to discourage me; they were meant to prepare me for the reality that I would have to fight for my place in every room I entered.

It wasn't fair, but it was the truth. And in the moments when I did have to work harder, when I saw others advance with half the effort, when my worth was questioned despite my qualifications, I understood exactly what she meant.

That realization came with weight. It was also what led me to choose education as a career. I knew firsthand the impact that a teacher's words could have—both the ones that uplifted and the ones that tore down. I had experienced moments when educators had doubted me, underestimated me, and tried to limit my potential. But I had also experienced the power of those who believed in me, who saw my worth, and who nurtured my talents. I wanted to be that kind of educator. I wanted to create classrooms where students—especially Black students—felt seen, valued, and capable of achieving anything they set their minds to. It meant sacrificing comfort for progress, trading in ease for excellence. It meant knowing that even on my best days, I would be held to a different standard, and that I had no choice but to exceed it. It meant that rest felt like laziness. That failure felt like falling behind, not just for myself but for everyone who had come before me. It meant that success was not just personal—it was communal. Every win I secured was for the ancestors who had been denied their own. Every step forward was for the ones who had been forced to stay still.

Ambition is often celebrated, but for Black men, it is also a burden. The price of ambition is not just the effort it takes to reach success but the constant push against forces that try to pull you back. It is knowing that you will always be scrutinized more harshly, questioned more often, and expected to prove yourself repeatedly in spaces where others are given the benefit of the doubt.

But ambition is also resilience. It is carrying the weight of history on your shoulders and refusing to let it hold you down. It is standing on the foundation built by those who came before you, knowing that every achievement is more than personal—it is a step forward for those who will follow. It means being hyper-aware of how you are perceived. It means constantly proving that you are more than a stereotype. It means never being allowed to simply *be*—because the moment you relax, the world is ready to count you out.

The world I grew up in—where my family and community poured into me—was a world built on affirmation and belief in my ability. But the world I was preparing for? That was something entirely different. It was a world where my intelligence could be dismissed. Where my accomplishments could be questioned. Where my presence in spaces could be seen as a surprise rather than an expectation.

Carrying that weight was both empowering and exhausting. On one hand, it made me sharp, disciplined, and unshakable in my determination. On the other hand, it often felt like I was being asked to perform for validation, to constantly prove my worth in ways that others were never required to.

But even with that weight, I have never let it crush me. Instead, I have let it fuel me. I have taken that fire and used it to push myself forward—to demand more, to expect more, and to create a life that was never meant to be handed to me, but one that I would claim as my own—passion, righteous anger, and the courage to take risks. It is the heat of ambition, the burn of injustice, and the boldness of stepping forward when the world tells you to stay put. It is the fire that drives me, challenges me, and forces me to rise.

I've never been the type to accept limits. From a young age, I wanted more—I wanted to be excellent, to exceed expectations, to prove that I belonged in any space I entered. But I learned early that passion alone wasn't enough—it had to be backed by action, by resilience, by an unshakable belief in my own potential.

One of my first encounters with this realization came in middle school. I had a dream of being a lawyer. I envisioned myself standing in a courtroom, presenting arguments with passion and conviction. I had watched enough legal dramas with my grandparents to be captivated by the power of language, the ability to advocate for others, and the idea of justice.

One day in class, I shared this aspiration. My teacher, a white woman, looked at me and, without hesitation, told me that it was unrealistic. That I should consider something "more practical." That the path to law was difficult, and maybe I should think about a trade instead.

I remember sitting there, feeling a mix of confusion and anger. It wasn't that she offered guidance—it was that she didn't see the potential in me to dream bigger. That moment wasn't just about law; it was about being told that my ambitions were too much. That my dreams were too far-fetched. It was a small comment to her, but to me, it was a defining moment. I was determined not just to prove her wrong, but to ensure that no one else had the power to place limits on my future. I hadn't said anything outrageous—I had simply dreamed out loud, naming ambitions that, in her eyes, weren't for me. She thought she was protecting me from disappointment, but I knew better.

That moment stayed with me—one that truly began to take shape in high school. By then, I had found my stride, stepping into leadership roles that would define my path. I immersed myself in extracurricular activities, serving as President of multiple clubs, President of the Student Council, and President of the Student Body. In 2010, I also had the honor of becoming the first Black Homecoming King in my school's history. That honor was not just personal—it was historic. My grandmother had been in the last graduating class of Bate High School, an all-Black segregated school, before it was closed and the community integrated Danville High School. Decades later, I stood as a symbol of progress, carrying her legacy forward in a place where Black students had once been excluded. It was a full-circle moment, a testament to how far we had come—and how far we still had to go.

My grandmother was always the first person to tell me I was special. Before I even understood what it meant to stand out, she made sure I knew that I carried something within me that the world needed to see. So, when I won Homecoming King, it wasn't just a title—it was a moment that affirmed everything she had ever told me about myself.

My school was majority white. Black students made up a fraction of the population, and leadership roles—whether in academics, athletics, or extracurricular activities—were often dominated by white students. Homecoming had historically been the same. The winners were usually the kids from well-known, white families—the ones whose parents were connected, who had deep roots in the community's legacy.

So, when I stood on that field and my name was called, it wasn't just my win. It was a win for every Black student who had felt unseen, for every student of color who had been told to stay in the background.

Being the first came with an unspoken burden. I couldn't just enjoy the moment—I had to carry it. I had to be mindful of how I carried myself, how I spoke, how I was perceived. Because I wasn't just representing myself—I was representing every Black student who had been overlooked before me. I knew that my presence alone challenged expectations, and for some, that was uncomfortable. Yet, I was created to make space for others to follow.

Winning Homecoming King was a triumph, but it wasn't without its challenges. I remember overhearing a conversation in the hallway—*'They just picked him because they wanted to make history.'* It wasn't about my leadership, my character, or my impact—it was reduced to a quota, a moment, a gesture. It stung, but it also reminded me of the reality I lived in. For some people, I would always have to justify my place. I had worked for this, just like I had worked for everything else in my life. And I wasn't about to let someone else's small-mindedness steal the joy of that moment.

I've never been the type to accept limits. From a young age, I wanted more—I wanted to be excellent, to exceed expectations, to prove that I belonged in any space I entered. But I learned early that passion alone wasn't enough—it had to be backed by action, by resilience, by an unshakable belief in my own potential.

Another occurrence of high school that I am reminded of is when I was denied an opportunity that I had worked for—one that I knew I had earned—only to watch it be handed to someone else, someone who looked different from me. I remember feeling the sting of unfairness, the heat rising in my chest. I wanted to yell, to demand an explanation, but I knew that wouldn't change anything. Instead, I made a decision: I would let my work speak louder than any excuse someone could give for overlooking me.

That experience taught me that anger doesn't have to be a weight—it can be a weapon.

Anger, when wielded with purpose, is not just about defiance—it is about transformation. It is about recognizing injustice and refusing to accept it as inevitable. It is about taking the heat of discrimination, doubt, and exclusion and forging something stronger out of it. I have learned that the anger I once carried as a child, the fire that burned when I was overlooked, is the same fire that drives me today.

Instead of letting it consume me, I have learned to channel it into action. High school became the proving ground where I turned my righteous anger into fuel. Every leadership position I took on, every speech I gave, every student I advocated for—it was all a part of ensuring that no one else would feel unseen the way I once had. I understood that leadership was not just about holding titles; it was about breaking barriers, setting new standards, and making space for others to follow. It was about ensuring that my achievements were not anomalies but stepping stones for those who would come after me. To let the world see the results of my determination rather than be distracted by the emotions behind it. Because if history has taught us anything, it is that those who change the world are often the ones who refuse to be silent in the face of injustice. It can be the thing that pushes you forward, forces you to sharpen yourself, and reminds you why you can't afford to slow down. I carried that lesson with me, using every moment of being doubted as motivation to excel beyond expectation.

During my senior year, I received my acceptance letter to the University of Louisville, accompanied by the prestigious Woodford R. Porter Scholarship. Named after the late Woodford R. Porter Sr., a former university trustee, the scholarship was created in 1984 to provide academic, personal, and professional support to its recipients. It upheld the four pillars of promise: scholarship, leadership, service, and heritage. At the time of my acceptance, the scholarship was a direct alignment with affirmative action initiatives—ensuring that students of color, particularly Black students, had access to higher education.

I remember sharing the news with a classmate, excited about what this opportunity meant for me and my family. Instead of congratulations, said, "You know you only got that scholarship because you're Black." Her words hit me like a slap. I had worked tirelessly to earn my place, to prove that I was worthy, yet in that moment, my achievement was diminished to nothing more than my identity. In that moment, I felt a mix of emotions—anger, frustration, disappointment—but mostly, exhaustion. It was the same fight I had been having my whole life, just in a different form. No matter how hard I worked, how many leadership roles I held, or how much I excelled, there would always be people who reduced my success to a handout rather than the result of my effort. My mother's words echoed in my mind: You will always have to work twice as hard to get half of what you deserve. And yet, even when I had done exactly that, I was still questioned. It was a painful reminder of the world I lived in—a world that often saw my success as unearned, despite the struggle behind every milestone.

I didn't say anything at that moment, but the words lingered with me. That night, I sat with the discomfort of knowing that no matter how hard I worked, some people would always assume that my success wasn't truly mine. It was a familiar narrative—the idea that Black success had to be justified, defended, explained. I told my mother what happened, and she simply nodded. 'You'll hear that more than once in your life, but don't ever let it make you small.' Those words became a guiding force for me. I carried them with me through every challenge, every victory. And when I stepped onto the campus of the University of Louisville as a Porter Scholar, I made a promise to myself: I would excel—not just for me, but for everyone who had been told they didn't belong.

Anger is often seen as destructive, but I've learned that when harnessed correctly, it is one of the most powerful fuels for change. There have been moments in my life when I've felt the heat of injustice, when I've seen doors close simply because of who I was. Some of those moments were subtle—microaggressions in academic spaces, assumptions made before I even opened my mouth. Others were blatant and undeniable, forcing me to face the reality that not all roads are paved the same way for everyone.

If there's one thing I've learned, it's that nothing great happens without risk. Some of the most defining moments of my life came not when I played it safe, but when I stepped into uncertainty, trusting that the fire inside me was enough to carry me through. I've learned that courage isn't about not being afraid—it's about acting with courage in spite of fear.

But courage is not just about standing up for yourself—it is about standing up for others, about creating space where there was none before. It is about recognizing that every bold step forward is an invitation for someone else to do the same. I have seen what happens when fear wins, when people hold back their voices, their dreams, their aspirations because the risk feels too great. And I have made a promise to myself that I will not be one of them.

Courage is often loud, but sometimes it is quiet—sometimes it is standing firm when everything in you wants to shrink back. I remember a moment in my senior year when a conversation in the hallway turned into something more. A few students were joking about race, about affirmative action, about who 'deserved' what. I could have walked away. I could have ignored it. But instead, I turned to them and said, "I worked for everything I have, just like you did. The only difference is, I had to prove it every step of the way." The conversation fell silent. I don't know if I changed their minds, but I knew I had spoken my truth. And sometimes, that is courage enough.

There have been moments when I questioned whether I was ready—whether I was capable, whether I belonged. And every time, I have been reminded that the fire inside of me is stronger than the fear trying to hold me back. It's about recognizing that the fire inside of you is stronger than the obstacles ahead. And every time I've taken that leap, I've found that I was more capable than I ever gave myself credit for.

Red is the color of action. It is the fire that refines, the heat that pushes me forward, the force that will not let me rest in mediocrity. Red is the fire that pushed me forward, but fire alone cannot sustain a person forever. It is passion. It is anger. It is courage. And it is mine. Because without fire, there is no transformation. Without heat, there is no strength. And without risk, there is no greatness.

Because fire does not exist without fuel, and ambition, anger, and courage have been mine. The flames had shaped me. They have shaped me, refined me, and carried me forward even when the path ahead was uncertain. But the thing about fire is that it does not burn forever—it must evolve, take on new forms, and find new meaning.

The flames of Red have pushed me forward, but the journey is not just about movement—it is about transformation. At some point, the flames must evolve, shift, and transform into something else. I had fought, I had proven myself, and I had broken barriers—but what happens after the battle? That's the question I had yet to answer.

Chapter 3: Yellow

Choosing Joy in the Midst of It All

Joy is often treated as something fleeting, a temporary burst of light that comes and goes. But I've come to realize that joy is not just a feeling—it's a practice, a choice, and sometimes even a form of resistance. In a world that often tells us to prepare for the worst, to brace ourselves for struggle, choosing joy is an act of defiance.

For so long, I viewed success as survival. I measured my progress in terms of what I had overcome, what I had endured, and what I had proven to others. But joy? That felt indulgent, almost selfish. I had been so conditioned to fight that I hadn't given myself permission to celebrate. I had mastered perseverance, but I had not yet mastered joy.

Joy is often overlooked in a world that prioritizes hustle and grinding over rest and reflection. Growing up, I was taught to chase success, to move from one achievement to the next without looking back. But joy requires pause. It requires us to stop, breathe, and take in the beauty of what we have accomplished. It asks us to revel in the warmth of what we have built, not just to keep building for the sake of progress.

Joy is also a reclamation. For so many of us, it has been taught that joy is secondary to survival, that it is something to be earned rather than something we are inherently deserving of. But I refuse to see joy as a privilege—I see it as a necessity. It is the very thing that reminds us we are alive, that we are whole, and that life is meant to be more than just hardship and perseverance. It is in the way we laugh, the way we dance, the way we allow ourselves to be fully present in the good moments rather than constantly bracing for the bad.

Joy has been found not only in personal reflection but also in the accomplishments that have shaped my journey. Every triumph has been a testament to perseverance, a milestone marking the journey from struggle to victory. I have learned to celebrate the wins—both big and small—because they represent the resilience, the work, and the determination it took to get here.

From becoming an Assistant Principal, then Principal, and later a university professor, I have found joy in guiding students, mentoring teachers, and shaping educational landscapes. One of my proudest moments was being recognized as one of Nashville's Black Top Forty Under 40, an honor that validated years of dedication, late nights, and unwavering persistence. It was a moment where I could pause and say, *"This is what hard work looks like. This is what joy in progress feels like."*

Writing and publishing my first book was another defining joy. To take my experiences, lessons, and insights and put them into words that could help others was one of the most fulfilling endeavors of my life. It was a moment of reflection, an acknowledgment that my voice mattered, that my perspective could help shape others on their own journeys. Seeing my work in the hands of readers, receiving messages from those who found resonance in my words—those were the moments where joy was no longer something abstract, but something tangible and real.

The recognition, the career milestones, the honors—they were all affirmations. But what truly brought me joy was the impact. The students who told me I made a difference in their lives. The teachers who carried what I taught them into their own classrooms. The communities that grew because of the work I was a part of. These moments remind me that success without joy is empty, but success that fuels joy is purpose fulfilled. Joy is found in triumph, but more importantly, it is found in knowing that those triumphs mean something beyond the accolades—they mean change, impact, and the kind of legacy I have always dreamed of building.

Joy is not a distraction from responsibility but a necessary component of a meaningful life. Without joy, accomplishments feel hollow, and struggles feel insurmountable. I've learned that joy does not erase hardship, but it provides the resilience to push through it. It is a force of renewal, a reminder that the work I do, the impact I have, and the life I live are not just about endurance but about fulfillment.

When I think of joy in its purest form, I think of childhood summers in Kentucky. Long, lazy afternoons spent outside, the sound of cicadas buzzing in the air, and the freedom of knowing that for just a little while, there were no worries. I remember running barefoot through the grass, playing with my brother, racing each other to the end of the street and back, only stopping when we couldn't breathe from laughter. It was in those moments that I understood joy as something instinctual, something that didn't need permission—it just existed. And yet, as I grew older, joy became something that felt harder to reach, something I had to justify. What changed? Was it the weight of responsibility? The expectation to constantly strive for the next goal? Somewhere along the way, I learned that joy wasn't something given—it was something we had to fight for.

I think back to family gatherings, the unspoken joy in the way my grandmother's house filled with laughter, the way music played in the background as everyone talked over each other, each voice rising in excitement. It wasn't just about the food on the table or the occasion itself—it was about the energy, the comfort, the shared history that made joy feel like a birthright. Those were the moments that, even in tough times, reminded me that joy is woven into our existence, a force that refuses to be overshadowed.

Even in moments of discipline, joy found its way into our home. My mother could correct us with a look, yet she'd be the first to tell a joke that left us laughing long after bedtime. My father, a man of strength and few words, carried joy in his own way—through the quiet pride in his work, through the way he would slip us extra treats when my mother wasn't looking, through the simple moments of watching a game together in silence, both of us knowing that words weren't always needed for joy to be felt.

Joy in my childhood was simple, effortless, boundless. It was running barefoot in the summer, playing without worry, finding happiness in the smallest of things. As I grew older, joy became more complex—something I had to work for, something I often postponed in favor of ambition. But now, I see joy differently. It is no longer just a fleeting feeling, but a practice, an intention, a commitment to myself.

Joy does not exist in isolation. It thrives in relationships, in the bonds we build, and in the spaces where we feel most seen and celebrated. Some of the greatest joys in my life have come not from my own accomplishments, but from the shared victories, the unbreakable camaraderie, the moments of laughter so deep they left me breathless. Community has always been a source of light, and friendships have been the lanterns guiding me through even my darkest moments.

There is a unique type of joy that exists in friendship—the kind that requires no explanation, no validation, just the simple comfort of being surrounded by people who love you as you are. I think of the times my closest friends and I sat around tables long after the meal was finished, swapping stories, reminiscing on the past, dreaming out loud about the future. The way laughter would erupt over inside jokes, the way our support for each other was unwavering. It is in those moments that I truly understood the power of joy—it is not just something we experience, but something we share.

Even in times of hardship, community has been my refuge. When I was exhausted, my friends reminded me to rest. When I doubted myself, they reminded me of my worth. Joy is magnified when it is shared, and I am grateful for the people in my life who have reminded me time and time again that I do not have to carry my burdens alone.

Burnout is the slow unraveling of joy, the gradual fading of light in the pursuit of something greater. I have felt it more times than I care to admit—the exhaustion that seeps into your bones, the numbness that replaces passion, the moments where even success feels like a burden. There was a time when I thought that working harder would fix everything, that if I just pushed through, joy would eventually return on its own. But joy is not something you stumble upon—it is something you must actively reclaim.

I remember the moment I realized I had lost my joy. I was accomplishing everything I had ever dreamed of, yet I felt nothing. My achievements felt hollow, my days blurred together, and I found myself constantly drained. It was in that space of exhaustion that I had to make a choice—either continue down a path that was breaking me, or step back and find my way back to the things that once brought me happiness.

I had to re-learn how to rest, how to set boundaries, how to take joy in the small things again. I started taking walks without my phone, simply observing the world around me. I reconnected with old hobbies that had nothing to do with work or productivity. I allowed myself to laugh without guilt, to take breaks without feeling like I was falling behind. Slowly, joy returned—not as a sudden burst, but as a steady presence. And with it came the understanding that burnout does not mean you have failed—it simply means you need to find your way back to yourself.

Joy, in many ways, was my inheritance. Even in the face of hardship, my ancestors found ways to laugh, to celebrate, to build moments of happiness that transcended their struggles. I think about my grandmother's stories of growing up in an all-Black school, of the pride they carried despite segregation. I think about my mother's voice singing gospel hymns in the kitchen, how those melodies filled our home with warmth. Joy was never separate from our history—it was an act of survival, a way to claim our space in a world that often tried to dim our light.

Sometimes, joy sneaks up on you when you least expect it. There was a time when I was having a particularly difficult day, weighed down by stress and responsibilities. I stopped at a coffee shop, just needing a moment to collect my thoughts, when I noticed a young child at the next table. She was coloring with absolute concentration, her small hands gripping a crayon with determination. When she noticed me watching, she held up her drawing and said, "It's for you!"

That simple moment caught me off guard. Here was a child who knew nothing of my stress, my deadlines, my endless to-do list, yet in that moment, she shared her joy freely. It was a reminder that joy does not always have to be earned—it can be given, received, and accepted without condition. I carried that drawing with me for weeks, a small but powerful reminder that even in the hardest moments, joy is always within reach.

The resilience of Black joy is unmatched. Despite historical oppression, despite systemic barriers, we continue to find ways to rejoice. From the rhythms of spirituals sung by those who came before us to the loud laughter of a Sunday dinner filled with family, our joy is an act of defiance. It's proof that no matter what, we refuse to be broken. This is why joy is more than just happiness—it is legacy.

This legacy of joy extends beyond my own family. It is seen in Black art, music, and literature—expressions of resilience wrapped in creativity. It is in the way we celebrate our wins loudly, in the way we dance unapologetically, in the way we turn even the simplest moments into reasons to rejoice. We carry joy in our bones, in our stories, in our traditions. It is a reminder that no matter how hard the world tries to take it from us, we will always find a way to reclaim it.

I have come to understand that joy is not the absence of struggle—it is what makes the struggle worthwhile. Every leadership position, every award, every classroom I've stepped into has been a reflection of the fire that once burned in me, pushing me forward even when I felt like stopping. I now recognize that joy is my right. It is in mentoring the next generation of educators, in seeing students grow into leaders, in using my voice to create meaningful change. It is in the moment I finally allowed myself to say, *"I have done enough. I am enough."*

I used to think joy was something you earned after the work was done. But now, I know that joy is the work. It is the thing that makes the struggle worthwhile, the thing that keeps me moving forward. It is in the way I choose to wake up each day with gratitude, the way I no longer wait for permission to celebrate myself, the way I see the beauty in where I've been and where I'm going.

I have learned that joy evolves. It shifts and reshapes itself as we grow. What once brought me joy may no longer serve me, and that is okay. The important thing is that I continue to seek it, to nurture it, to make space for it. I no longer wait for the perfect moment to experience happiness—I claim it in the everyday moments, in the laughter of friends, in the quiet mornings before the world wakes up, in the knowledge that I am exactly where I need to be.

Joy is not just the reward at the end of the journey—it is the journey itself. And as I move forward, I carry that truth with me, holding onto the light, choosing to celebrate, and embracing every moment of joy that life has to offer.

Because joy is not a reward—it is my right.

Yellow is the color of sunshine, of warmth, of celebration. It is the reminder that even in the midst of challenges, there is still light. And as I move forward, I am choosing to hold onto that light. I am choosing to celebrate. I am choosing joy.

Joy must be cultivated and protected. It requires intention, the willingness to step away from exhaustion, and the courage to embrace happiness even in a world that often discourages it. Joy is in the laughter shared with friends, in the quiet moments of peace, in the triumph of choosing oneself. It is in knowing that we are not only surviving—we are thriving.

As I continue to build my career, to grow in my purpose, I no longer see joy as an afterthought. It is central to the life I want to live. I will honor it, nurture it, and allow it to guide me as fiercely as ambition once did. Because at the end of the day, what good is success if it isn't accompanied by joy?

Chapter 4: Gray
The In-Between: Navigating Self-Doubt and Imposter Syndrome

Self-doubt finds its way in through the cracks, whispering that maybe this is all temporary, that maybe at any moment, someone will figure out that I don't deserve to be here. That the achievements, the recognition, the milestones—all of it—were flukes. It is an internal battle that many successful people face, but for Black professionals, it carries a different weight. It is not just the fear of personal failure, but the unspoken reality that when we falter, it is not just an individual loss—it is proof to some that we never should have been given a seat at the table in the first place.

I have felt this weight in many rooms, in many seasons of my life. But I also know that doubt is not an indication of failure—it is often a sign of growth. To be in the Gray is to be in transition, to be learning, evolving, and stepping into something greater. It is uncomfortable, but it is necessary.

The first time I truly felt like I didn't belong wasn't in college or during my professional career—it was much earlier, in my K-12 education. There is a unique kind of isolation that comes with being a high-achieving Black student in predominantly white spaces. The feeling of being both seen and unseen. I was expected to be excellent, to represent something larger than myself, but also reminded—sometimes subtly, sometimes overtly—that I was an outsider.

I was in an Honors Math Course in the seventh grade, a space where I was not only expected to excel but to prove that I deserved to be there. I was the only Black student in that class, a fact that became evident every time we split into groups or engaged in classroom discussions. In some ways, it was empowering—I was a trailblazer, a representation of what was possible. But in other ways, it was isolating.

I was constantly aware that I had to be twice as prepared, twice as articulate, and twice as composed as my peers. Numbers had always made sense to me—math was my comfort zone, a subject where logic ruled and emotions didn't get in the way. But that comfort quickly faded when I noticed how my presence seemed to unsettle both my teacher and my classmates.

One afternoon, the teacher asked a particularly difficult question, and I knew the answer. My hand shot up. I had calculated the problem in my head faster than anyone else. But the teacher hesitated before calling on me. Instead, she glanced around the room, scanning for another hand. Only when no one else volunteered did she sigh and say, "Okay, Bryson, let's see what you've got." When I shared my answers, my teacher furrowed her brow, scrutinizing my work in a way she never did with my white classmates.

"Are you sure about that?" she asked, her voice laced with skepticism. The doubt in her voice stung. When I answered correctly, she seemed almost surprised. I nodded, standing firm in my response. Instead of praising my problem-solving skills, she said, "Hmm, well, even a broken clock is right twice a day." The classroom erupted in awkward laughter. My stomach tightened, my face burned with humiliation. I knew what she was implying: I wasn't supposed to be here. I wasn't supposed to be excelling. I wasn't supposed to make them uncomfortable with my intelligence. She then turned to another student—a white student—who had arrived at a similar answer but had taken longer to solve it. "Great job, Michael," she praised him, while barely acknowledging my effort.

I overheard whispers— "Do you think he really did that on his own?" "He probably got lucky." "Maybe the teacher is giving him a break." That was the moment I realized that being right wasn't always enough—not when you were the only one in the room who looked like you. I started questioning myself more, second-guessing my abilities, and wondering if my place in that classroom was ever truly secure.

For the first time, I felt the sharp sting of imposter syndrome, not because I lacked ability, but because the world around me was unwilling to see my brilliance. This experience mirrored what so many Black students face in honors courses and Advanced Placement programs. It wasn't just about the difficulty of the subject matter—it was about navigating a space that wasn't designed for you to thrive, about constantly proving your intelligence in a way that others didn't have to.

The education system, for all its promises of opportunity and advancement, can also be a place where self-doubt takes root. The way students are spoken to, the way they are categorized, the way expectations are subtly (or not so subtly) communicated—these things matter.

For many Black students, school is a place where they are constantly reminded that they must work twice as hard for half the recognition. There were moments when I was praised, but the praise always carried an undertone of surprise, as if excellence from someone like me was an anomaly.

Like middle school, I was often the only or one of three Black students in Advanced Placement courses in high school. I remember one particular moment in an Advanced Placement English class when we were discussing *To Kill a Mockingbird*. The class conversation turned toward race, and suddenly, all eyes were on me. It was an unspoken expectation that I would offer the "Black perspective," as if I were a spokesperson rather than just another student. It was a subtle but powerful reminder that I was different, that I did not fully belong in the way my white peers did.

No, it wasn't fair. But fairness has never been part of the equation. The reality is, when you're one of the few, you don't get to be just an individual—you become a symbol, whether you want to or not. And at 16, that weight was heavy. I wasn't elected to be a spokesperson for my entire race, but at that moment, it felt like I was. The pattern was familiar—the unspoken expectation that I had to justify my presence in those spaces.

My white classmates gave me cautious glances, some outright avoiding eye contact. My teacher, instead of encouraging discussion, quickly pivoted to another student, as if my perspective made the conversation too uncomfortable.

Later that day, a classmate pulled me aside and whispered, "You don't have to make everything about race, you know." I was stunned. The novel we were discussing literally revolved around issues of race, injustice, and oppression, yet my thoughts were deemed excessive—too much, too uncomfortable. That moment made me hyper-aware of how often Black students are expected to silence themselves for the comfort of others. It wasn't just about intelligence or work ethic—it was about navigating the invisible rules of how much Blackness was "acceptable" in predominantly white spaces.

It's experiences like these that plant the seeds of self-doubt, forcing students like me to constantly question: Am I speaking too much? Am I doing too much? Am I allowed to take up space? There was also the time I was selected for a leadership position, only to overhear a peer say, "They probably just picked him to check a box." The implication being that my abilities were not enough—there had to be another reason I was chosen.

That moment solidified something I had always felt—that no matter how hard I worked, how much I achieved, or how well I performed, there would always be those who saw me not as an individual, but as a token. It was a painful realization, but also a defining one. Because rather than letting it break me, I used it as fuel to prove, over and over again, that I belonged.

When I became an educator, I thought I had left those doubts behind. I had earned my place in the classroom, I had proven myself. But imposter syndrome does not fade just because the title on your door changes. I was typically the only Black teacher or the only Black male teacher in every school I worked in. Being one of the few Black male educators in every school I worked at meant two things:

1. I was both hyper-visible and invisible at the same time.
2. I was regularly expected to "handle" Black students when they stepped out of line.

That meant I wasn't just an educator—I was also a cultural bridge, an unspoken disciplinarian, and an unofficial mentor to students who saw themselves in me. My presence was both a source of pride and an unspoken burden. I was regularly tapped to "handle" Black students when they were out of line. "Can you talk to him? He's just not responding to me," white teachers would often say about Black boys who were struggling in class. The assumption was that I could "relate" to them in ways my white colleagues could not—yet I was never called upon in the same way for white students. It was a pattern that reinforced how I was perceived—not just as an educator, but as a figure meant to "manage" certain students rather than nurture all students equally.

At almost every school, there was an unspoken rule: whenever a Black male student got in trouble, they would send him to me. Not because I was a leader, not because I had a rapport with him, but because they thought I was the "Black Whisperer." At first, I embraced the role—because I did connect with those students in a way that others didn't. But over time, I realized how problematic it was. Why was it my responsibility to "fix" them? Why weren't these teachers reflecting on their own biases and how they contributed to student disengagement?

I remember one particular situation where a Black male student had an argument with his teacher—a white woman who, instead of de-escalating, escalated the situation further. The moment I walked into the room, she turned to me and said, "Can you deal with your kids?" Her words cut deep. Your kids. As if I was not an administrator like her, but a handler, responsible for controlling the "problem" students. No one ever asked my white colleagues to 'handle' white students.

I walked the student out into the hallway, ignoring the stares, and I let him talk. The anger in his voice softened as he realized I wasn't there to punish him—I was there to listen. By the time we were done, he was calm, ready to return to class. That's what culturally responsive education looks like. But my white colleagues didn't see it that way. Instead, they said, "You go too easy on them." What they failed to understand was that discipline without dignity is just oppression.

As I transitioned into administration, these issues became even more apparent. As an Assistant Principal, I was now in a position of leadership—but that didn't mean I was respected. As a first year Assistant Principal, I faced even greater challenges. I was the only Black male in leadership at a school dominated by white women, white families, and white children. In a school filled with white administrators, white teachers, and mostly white families, my presence was not celebrated—it was scrutinized. My credentials and experience were often overlooked or questioned, and I felt the weight of being treated as an outsider in my own school. I felt the weight of my existence every single day.

I was spoken over in meetings.

Ideas I proposed were dismissed—until a white colleague repeated them.

Parents would bypass me, assuming I was a disciplinarian, not an academic leader.

Black staff members saw how I was treated—how my authority was undermined, how my presence was tolerated rather than embraced, how I was often left out of key decision-making conversations, and how my decisions were constantly second-guessed. One of them pulled me aside and warned me: "You have to be careful. They're watching you differently than they watch everyone else." Another day, a Black teacher pulled me aside and said, "We see how they treat you. Just know you're not crazy." I hadn't realized how much I needed to hear that until I did.

Every day, I had to walk a tightrope—being strong enough to withstand the pressure, but not so strong that I was labeled "aggressive."

Being vocal enough to advocate for my students, but not so vocal that I was seen as "difficult." It was exhausting.

And yet, despite all of this, I endured. Because I knew that if I left, the space would be even more homogenous than before. I stayed, not because it was easy, but because I refused to let them erase me.

Discrimination was not always loud, but it was always present, and I had to navigate it carefully, knowing that any pushback could be perceived as aggression. There was no room for mistakes. No space for vulnerability. The burden of being a Black leader in a predominantly white institution meant that every action was scrutinized, every decision had higher stakes, and every misstep—no matter how small—was amplified.

This wasn't just my experience—it was a systemic issue. Black male educators and administrators are rare, not because we lack the skills or ambition, but because the system isn't designed for us to thrive. From my published article in K12 Digest, I have spoken extensively on the need for more Black male educators in school leadership. The experience of being a Black male educator in a predominantly white school system is not unique to me. Research shows that Black male educators make up less than 2% of the teaching workforce. Schools often fail to support and retain Black teachers once they enter the system.

In my published article, I discussed how pipeline programs for Black male educators need more than just recruitment efforts—they need retention strategies that focus on mentorship, leadership pathways, and protection against systemic bias.

One of the biggest challenges for Black male educators is the lack of upward mobility. Many are seen as "good disciplinarians" but not considered for leadership roles like principal or district administrator. The assumption is that we can control students but not lead entire schools.

In my own journey, I saw this play out firsthand. I had more degrees than some of my peers, more leadership experience, and yet, I was overlooked for positions I was qualified for—replaced by white colleagues with less experience. But as I wrote in my article, representation at the leadership level is essential. When students of color see Black male educators in leadership positions, it expands their vision of success. They see that intelligence, authority, and power can look like them too.

Black male educators must have mentorship and advocacy to navigate the unspoken challenges of leadership in predominantly white spaces. Also, it is essential that schools actively work to dismantle biases in hiring, promotion, and retention practices to create a true community. In my experience, students—especially Black students— gravitated toward me not because I was an administrator, but because I was someone they saw as an advocate. Someone who understood what it meant to navigate a school system that was not designed with them in mind.

As I look back on my career in K-12, I realize that my experiences were not unique. The struggles I faced were the same struggles countless Black male educators endure. But despite the challenges, I remained in the fight—not just for myself, but for the students who needed to see that they, too, could belong in these spaces.

Gray is the in-between. It is doubt, uncertainty, and waiting to see if all the work will be worth it. Gray is not just uncertainty—it is transformation. It is the space where growth happens, where resilience is built, where we learn to trust ourselves even when the path is unclear. Gray is every moment I questioned if I belonged. Gray is every time I had to fight twice as hard just to be seen. Gray is the exhaustion of proving myself over and over again.

But Gray is also where I learned resilience. Because even when self-doubt crept in, even when the system tried to diminish me, I did not disappear. Gray taught me that belonging is not something granted—it is something you claim. And I claimed my space.

I have learned to make peace with the Gray. To understand that doubt does not mean I am unqualified, and fear does not mean I am incapable. Because the truth is, I belong here. And no amount of self-doubt will change that.

Chapter 5: Blue

Healing, Self-Worth, and the Cost of Carrying It All

Blue is the color of stillness, the color of depth, the color that forces you to face yourself without distractions. It is the color of clarity, the deep exhale after years of holding your breath, the peace that comes when you finally realize that you don't have to prove yourself anymore.

For so long, I had measured my worth by how much I could carry. I took pride in my resilience, in my ability to push through exhaustion, in the fact that no matter how tired, drained, or overwhelmed I was, I kept going. I thought that was the definition of strength. But what I didn't realize was that sometimes, true strength is knowing when to put it all down.

Healing isn't just about getting over the past. It's about recognizing how the past still shapes you, how the things you've been through affect the way you see yourself, the way you move through the world, and most of all, the way you define your own worth. I spent years chasing validation, thinking that if I achieved enough, worked hard enough, and proved myself enough, then I would finally feel whole. But the truth is, self-worth isn't something you earn—it's something you already have. The problem was, I didn't know that yet.

I remember the night I should have felt proud. It was one of those big, career-defining moments—the kind of night that was supposed to feel like a culmination of everything I had worked for. I had just been named one of Nashville's Black Forty Under 40, an honor recognizing young Black professionals who had made a significant impact in their fields.

It was supposed to be a celebration, a moment of recognition. The culmination of years of hard work, sacrifice, and resilience. The kind of moment that younger me would have looked forward to, proof that all the long nights, all the extra effort, and all the times I had pushed myself past exhaustion had been worth it.

The room was filled with applause, the kind of slow, congratulatory nods from colleagues who recognized what it meant to be standing where I was. I shook hands, took photos, smiled when I was supposed to smile. But as I walked off the stage, holding the plaque with my name etched into it, I felt… empty. Not just a little underwhelmed. Completely hollow.

I went home that night, placed the award on my desk, and sat in silence. The walls of my home, usually a refuge, felt suffocating. I picked up my phone, scrolling through the congratulatory messages, but none of it felt real. I should have been celebrating. I should have felt fulfilled.

Instead, I felt like I was standing at the peak of a mountain, only to realize I had been climbing the wrong one. That night, I asked myself a question I had never dared to before: *"Who am I if I'm not achieving?"* And for the first time in my life, I didn't have an answer.

Growing up, I was taught that hard work was a virtue, that you prove your worth through what you produce. And I took that lesson and ran with it. I was the student who never settled for less than an A, the one who took on leadership roles, the one who was always "going places." My family praised me for my ambition, my drive, my ability to push forward. But no one ever taught me how to just be.

I learned how to chase the next thing, but I never learned how to sit with myself. There's a specific kind of exhaustion that comes with never feeling like you can stop. Even in moments of success, I was always thinking about the next step. I would accomplish one goal, only to immediately move the finish line further away. It wasn't just ambition—it was survival.

Because when you've been told your whole life that you have to work twice as hard to get half as much, stopping feels like falling behind. I had spent so much of my life proving myself in rooms where I was often the only one who looked like me. I worked twice as hard, not just because I wanted to, but because I felt like I had to. I wanted to belong. I wanted to be seen as worthy. And it worked. Until it didn't.

As a first-generation college student, the pressure wasn't just internal—it was generational. I wasn't just succeeding for myself; I was succeeding for my family, my community, and everyone who had sacrificed before me so I could be where I was. There was an unspoken expectation that I had to make it because failure wasn't an option.

Being the first to do something is a complicated kind of honor. On one hand, it's a source of pride—to know that you've broken barriers, that you're paving the way for those who come after you. But on the other hand, it's isolating. There's no blueprint, no guidebook, no safety net.

I remember sitting in lecture halls, surrounded by classmates whose parents had attended college, whose families had the experience and knowledge to guide them through. I didn't have that. While I had incredibly supportive parents, I was figuring it out as I went, stumbling through financial aid forms, course selections, and career planning on my own. And even though I had mentors, the weight of expectation never left me. I wasn't just earning a degree—I was proving something.

I was the "golden child"—the one who was supposed to "make it." The one who, from a young age, was told I was "different," that I had a bright future, that I was the one who would change things. That kind of praise feels good at first, but over time, it becomes a cage. Because when people see you as the one who will succeed, there's no room for failure.

I felt like I couldn't make mistakes, couldn't fall short, couldn't ever let anyone down. The idea of disappointing my family, my mentors, my community—it was suffocating. There was this unspoken rule: If I slowed down, if I took a break, if I admitted that I was struggling—it would mean I was wasting my potential. I wasn't allowed to be tired. I wasn't allowed to be unsure. I wasn't allowed to be anything less than exceptional.

And that's the thing about being the golden child—your accomplishments become your identity. People don't just celebrate what you do; they start defining you by it. You're not seen as a person—you're seen as potential. And what happens when you start questioning that potential? What happens when the golden child no longer wants to carry the weight?

For a long time, I didn't allow myself to ask those questions. Because to ask them meant admitting that I was exhausted. That I wasn't sure if all of this effort would ever be enough. That no matter how much I achieved, there was always more.

The problem with being the golden child is that people expect you to always shine. But what happens when you start to dim? What happens when you realize that you don't want to be a symbol—you just want to be human? Because no amount of degrees, titles, or awards can fill a void that is built on the need for approval.

Healing isn't just about rest—it's about learning when to let go. And sometimes, letting go feels like loss. I had spent years carrying everything—expectations, responsibilities, and the unspoken pressure to always perform. But the strongest thing I ever did was stop. It wasn't one dramatic event that made me realize I was exhausted—no breaking point, no single moment of collapse. It was much quieter than that. It crept in slowly, over time, disguised as normalcy. It was in the way I would sit in my car for too long after arriving home, staring at the dashboard, not yet ready to step inside. It was in the way I would wake up feeling like I had already failed the day before it even began. It was in the way every accomplishment felt like just another checkmark on an endless to-do list—never enough, never fulfilling, never the validation. I had once hoped it would be.

A year after the Nashville's Black Forty Under 40, I reached another milestone—Interim Principal. I finally had accomplished a goal that I had reached for my entire career. And then, one night, after another long day of doing everything I was "supposed" to do, I sat in my office and felt nothing. I had spent years moving from one goal to the next, barely stopping to breathe. Always reaching, always climbing, always trying to prove something—though I wasn't always sure to whom. And for what? The accolades, the promotions, the recognition—I had them all. By all definitions, I was successful. I had worked hard, I had built a career, I had proven myself. But sitting there in the quiet, staring at the awards I had collected over the years, I felt unfulfilled. Not just tired. Hollow.

I thought about the sacrifices I had made to get here—the sleepless nights, the missed moments with family and friends, the times

I had swallowed my own exhaustion because I believed the payoff would be worth it. And now that I had finally "made it," I was confronted with a truth I had been avoiding for years: This isn't enough.

Because the truth is, nothing will ever be enough when you are chasing validation. I picked up one of the awards—one that, not long ago, I would have considered a pinnacle of success. I turned it over in my hands, feeling its weight, tracing the engraved letters of my name. And I asked myself a question I had never dared to before: *"Who am I if I'm not achieving?"* For the first time in my life, I didn't have an answer.

I sat there, grappling with the terrifying realization that I had built my entire identity around external validation. That my worth had always been tied to what I could accomplish. That I had spent my whole life proving myself—to teachers, to colleagues, to family, to society. But at that moment, there was no one left to prove myself to. And the silence was deafening.

As I sat there, I thought back to a conversation I had with a mentor years ago. He had asked me a simple question: "If you weren't doing what you do now, who would you be?" At the time, I had laughed it off, giving a half-hearted answer about always finding a way to succeed. But now, the weight of that question settled on me in a way I wasn't ready for. Because I didn't know.

I had spent my life so focused on climbing, on proving, on earning my place, that I had never actually stopped to think about who I was outside of the climb. Who was I without the titles? Who was I without the next big goal? Who was I if no one was watching?

And for the first time, I realized I didn't have an identity outside of my achievements. That night, as I stared at the trophies, the degrees, the certificates—things I had once believed would make me feel whole—I felt something shift inside me. A quiet truth, one that had been waiting for me to finally acknowledge it: Self-worth isn't something you earn. It isn't something you collect through achievements. It isn't something you chase. It is something that has always existed within you, waiting for you to recognize it.

But I hadn't recognized it. Because I had spent my whole life believing that if I wasn't moving, I was failing. That if I wasn't achieving, I wasn't enough. And now, I had no idea what to do next.

There is something terrifying about realizing you have spent your entire life running and have no idea how to stop.

I wanted to rest. I wanted to breathe. But how do you teach yourself to slow down when you have spent years convincing yourself that your value is in your productivity? I wanted to believe that I was enough without the awards, without the success, without the validation of others. But did I?

I had spent so long measuring my worth by what I could produce—how could I unlearn that? How could I let go of something that had defined me for so long? The truth is, I didn't know. But I knew one thing for certain: I couldn't keep living like this. Something had to change.

That night, for the first time, I allowed myself to imagine a different way of being. A life that wasn't dictated by my to-do list. A version of myself that wasn't constantly chasing approval. I didn't know what that life looked like yet. But for the first time, I was willing to find out.

I remember the first time I actively chose rest. It wasn't just a weekend off or a quick vacation. It was a conscious decision to step away from the need to prove myself. And it was terrifying. The first few days, I felt restless. I kept reaching for my phone, feeling like I was falling behind. I convinced myself that if I wasn't busy, I was failing.

But the more I sat in the stillness, the more I realized how exhausted I had been.

I had to redefine success. I had to sit in silence and ask myself the questions I had always avoided: *"What do I enjoy when I'm not chasing goals? What makes me happy outside of success? Who am I when no one is watching?"* And let me tell you—answering those questions was one of the hardest things I've ever done. Because for a long time, I didn't know. But healing? Healing meant giving myself permission to figure it out.

It wasn't easy, but I realized something: If I had spent years proving myself, then I could also spend years healing. Healing meant unlearning years of toxic productivity. It meant choosing myself, even when it felt selfish. It meant recognizing that I didn't need to be in a constant state of motion to be valuable. And most importantly—it meant understanding that I deserved peace.

For so long, I had measured my worth by how much I could carry. I took pride in my resilience, in my ability to push through exhaustion, in the fact that no matter how tired, drained, or overwhelmed I was, I kept going.

But I have come to learn that self-worth isn't about endurance—it's about knowing when to let go. I no longer live for validation. I no longer seek worth in my accomplishments. I am enough—just as I am.

Because self-worth isn't something you earn. It's something you already have. And for the first time, I'm finally seeing myself clearly.

Chapter 6: Pink
The Journey of Self-Love and Embracing All That I Am

I can remember as a child, one Christmas, I received an art set. It was the kind of gift that made my eyes widen—a box filled with endless colors, markers, pencils, and paints. A world of possibility contained within its neatly packed trays.

A day or two after Christmas, one of my older maternal cousins came over to my house. We sat together, flipping through blank pages, carefully choosing colors, sketching out our imaginations onto the paper. My father was also present, watching from across the room.

At one point, Daddy asked my cousin what his favorite color was. Without hesitation, he replied, "Blue." Daddy nodded, turning to me. "What about you?" I picked up a pink marker and smiled. "Pink." My cousin snickered. Daddy let out a small laugh, shaking his head. "Of course, you would like pink," he said.

They laughed together, an inside joke I didn't fully understand. But I knew enough to recognize that it was about me. About what I had just admitted. About the color I had chosen.

For the first time, I felt like I had picked the wrong answer. I didn't know why, but I could feel it in the way they reacted—that pink wasn't the "right" choice. That pink meant something about me that I wasn't supposed to say out loud. It was a small moment. One that most people wouldn't even remember. But I never forgot. Because that was the day I learned that who I was could be something to be laughed at.

By the time I reached high school, I had learned how to play the role well. I was respected. I was a leader. I excelled academically, and my success was praised. But even as I succeeded, I was still seeking something deeper—something I didn't yet have the words for. Love.

Acceptance. A sense of belonging that wasn't contingent on performance.

The "Golden Child" syndrome followed me everywhere. I was the one who was going places. The one who was always making his family proud. The one who was supposed to have everything figured out. But the thing about being the Golden Child is that you rarely get the space to be human.

I felt like I was always being watched. Always expected to be the best version of myself. Always aware that my wins weren't just mine—they were for my family, my community, my people. I had to be excellent. Because anything less than excellence was failure. And when you carry that kind of pressure for too long, it becomes exhausting.

I wasn't just striving for success—I was desperate for it. Because I thought success would finally make me feel worthy.
But the thing about external validation is that it is never enough. No award, no title, no amount of praise could fill the void that came from never learning how to validate myself. Because what happens when you achieve everything you thought you needed to feel whole—and you still feel empty?

From a young age, I learned what Black masculinity was supposed to look like. Strong. Tough. Unshakable. Black boys are often taught, whether explicitly or implicitly, that to show vulnerability is to invite weakness, and to invite weakness is to invite destruction. "Man up." "Stop acting soft." "What you crying for?" "You better not let them see you weak." The message was always clear—real men don't break. They endure. They tough it out. They don't show emotion unless it's anger. And for Black men, there was an additional layer of expectation.

The world already saw us as threats. As dangerous. As criminals. As inherently aggressive. So, we had to be even more controlled, even more composed, even more careful. I quickly learned that boys like me were not always safe in Black spaces. I wasn't bullied, but I was corrected. I wasn't ostracized, but I was *taught*—through jokes, through teasing, through silent glances—that my softness needed to be managed.

So, I adapted. I deepened my voice when I felt it was too high. I took up space in a way that was "acceptable." I learned to laugh along with the jokes—even when they were about me. Because being too soft as a Black man could make you a target. For rejection. For violence. For dismissal. For ridicule. And so, I tucked away the parts of me that didn't fit into the mold I was given. But when you shrink yourself to fit, you lose pieces of who you really are.

As I grew older, I began to realize that my struggle wasn't just about masculinity. It was about who I was as a whole. I was a Black man. I was a Black man with other identities. I was an academic, a leader, a professional navigating spaces where I was often the only one who looked like me. Each of those identities came with expectations, pressures, and responsibilities.

I had learned how to move through Black spaces carefully ensuring that my "whole self" was never too visible, never too apparent. I had learned how to move through predominantly white spaces carefully ensuring that my Blackness was palatable, that my confidence was never mistaken for aggression. I had learned how to code-switch, shapeshift, and adapt so well that I started to lose track of who I was underneath it all.

But who was I when I wasn't performing? Who was I when I wasn't seeking approval? When wasn't I proving myself? Who was I when I allowed myself to just be? There is no exhaustion quite like having to prove yourself in two worlds at the same time.

In white spaces, I was too Black. In Black spaces, I was too different. And somehow, in both places, I was expected to be exceptional just to be accepted. For as long as I can remember, I have been caught between these two realities—performing, adjusting, shrinking, expanding, trying to take up space, yet not take up too much space. Because the world already told me that as a Black man, I had to work twice as hard to get half as much. That my excellence had to be undeniable—a shield against racism, discrimination, and doubt.

Every Black person in a predominantly white space knows what it feels like to be "the only one." The only Black person in the room. The only Black man on the panel. The only Black student in the AP class. The only Black faculty member in the meeting. The only Black administrator at the leadership table.

Being "the only one" means carrying an unspoken weight—the weight of representation, the pressure to be flawless, because if you make a mistake, it won't just be seen as an individual failure. It will be seen as confirmation of every stereotype they already believe about us.

So, you sit up straighter. You speak carefully, because passion can be mistaken for aggression. You laugh when you want to correct someone's offensive comment. You bite your tongue when they tokenize you, when they ask you to be the voice of all Black people in the room. You work twice as hard to be half as respected.

And when you finally achieve something undeniable—when you secure the title, the degree, the award, the position—they still question you. "Are you sure you belong here?" "You must have had some help getting in." "You're so articulate." The code-switching, the performance, the careful curation of your presence—it becomes exhausting.

But just when you think you can relax among your own, another battle begins. No one prepared me for the struggle of proving myself in my own community. I thought Black spaces would be safe. That they would be where I could rest. But sometimes, rest was just another battle. Because I quickly learned that not all Black lives matter in our community.

There is an unspoken truth in our community that we don't always want to talk about: Some Black people only feel connected to you if your Blackness matches theirs. And if it doesn't? If you move differently, speak differently, love differently, show up differently? You become an outsider in your own home.

For some Black boys, who never quite fit the mold, rejection didn't come in one big moment—it came in small, subtle ways that taught them that belonging was conditional.
They learn that:

If you didn't play sports, you weren't "one of the guys."

If your voice wasn't deep enough, your presence wasn't respected.

If you were too soft, too sensitive, too expressive—you were a joke.

If you were identified as queer, your Blackness was questioned.

There were times when I felt safer in white spaces, not because they were welcoming, but because at least I already knew I was an outsider. But to feel like an outsider among your own people? That is a different kind of heartbreak. To be told that you don't belong among the very people who should embrace you. To be told that your Blackness isn't enough because it isn't packaged the way they expect. That is a wound that doesn't heal easily.

I reached a breaking point. I realized that if I had to keep proving myself just to be accepted, then maybe those spaces were never meant for me in the first place. If my Blackness was up for debate in my own community, then maybe it was time to redefine community. And that's when I stopped trying to fit in.

I stopped shrinking myself to fit into Black spaces that told me I wasn't "Black enough." I stopped overperforming in white spaces just to convince them I was "worthy." I stopped carrying the exhaustion of constantly proving myself. Because I had spent too much time asking for permission to exist. I didn't need validation. I didn't need approval. I didn't need to fit into anyone's definition of Blackness—except my own. And that? That was the beginning of my healing.

The greatest lie we were ever told is that there is only one way to be Black. Blackness is not a singular experience. It is vast. It is fluid. It is diverse. Blackness includes:

The queer kids who don't feel safe coming out in their own families.

The quiet Black boys who didn't fit in with the athletes.

The Black men who love poetry, art, and music instead of football and basketball.

The Black girls who were told they were "too aggressive" for being passionate.

The Black children who grew up in private schools, feeling like they had to "code-switch" just to come home.

ALL Black lives matter. Not just the ones that fit the mold. We need to do better for our own people. Because Black kids shouldn't have to fight for acceptance from the world and their own community. To the parents reading this:

Give your children space to be who they are.

Let them color outside the lines.

If your son likes pink, let him like pink.

If your daughter loves science instead of dolls, encourage her.

If your child is different, let them be different without shame.

The way you respond to your child's authenticity shapes their entire life. Don't laugh at them when they show you who they are. Don't dismiss their emotions just because the world taught you to be tough. Don't make them feel like they have to change to earn your love. Because they will carry that wound for years.

And trust me, healing from childhood rejection is one of the hardest things to unlearn. Let your children be free. Let them explore. Let them exist without needing to prove anything to you. Because love should never be something they have to earn.

I spent years trying to fit into spaces that weren't meant for me. Years seeking approval from people who were never going to give it. But I don't seek approval anymore. I don't shrink myself. I don't tone myself down. I show up fully, unapologetically, and without fear. Because I belong, exactly as I am. No more proving. No more asking for permission. I am enough. I always was.

Chapter 7: Green

The Evolution of Who I Am Becoming

Growth is a process, not a place. It isn't a straight path with a clear destination—it's a winding road with unexpected turns, pauses, and moments of uncertainty. For the longest time, I thought growth meant moving forward at all costs, pushing past obstacles, and never looking back. But what I've come to realize is that true growth isn't just about *moving*—it's about *becoming*.

Becoming means learning to sit with yourself, to reflect on your past without being bound by it, and to embrace the person you are stepping into. It means recognizing that you are allowed to change, to shift, to evolve in ways that may surprise even you.

For a long time, I resisted change—not because I didn't want to grow, but because I was afraid of what growth might cost me. Would I lose people? Would I lose myself? Would I have to let go of the security that came with being who I had always been?

We don't always talk about how unsettling growth can be. Sometimes, it feels like standing in front of a mirror and not quite recognizing the reflection staring back at you. You start to see parts of yourself that you didn't notice before—some beautiful, some broken, some still in progress. Growth is about learning to embrace all of those parts, to integrate them into the person you are becoming, rather than shaming yourself for who you once were.

I have spent so much of my life striving—striving to prove myself, striving to belong, striving to be enough. And what I've come to understand is that sometimes, growth isn't about striving at all. Sometimes, growth is about *shedding*.

Growth requires a shedding—a necessary release of the layers we once carried, the roles we once played, and the identities we once clung to for survival. It is a process of unlearning, of questioning, of standing in the mirror and asking, *"Who am I without all the titles, expectations, and external affirmations?"*

For much of my life, I defined myself by what I achieved. I wore my accomplishments like armor, believing that they protected me from rejection, from self-doubt, from the creeping fear that maybe—just maybe—who I was at my core wasn't enough. I built my identity around resilience, around strength, around the idea that as long as I kept pushing forward, I was proving my worth. But what happens when the armor gets too heavy?

For years, I carried the weight of perfectionism, the weight of being the one who "made it," the weight of being a Black man in predominantly white spaces, a "different" man in Black spaces, and an overachiever in every space in between. And while I took pride in my ability to navigate these worlds, I never stopped to ask myself if I actually *wanted* to keep carrying it all.

Shedding old identities isn't easy. It means confronting the parts of yourself that were created out of necessity, not authenticity. It means looking at the labels that were placed on you and asking if they still serve you. It means acknowledging that just because something once fit, doesn't mean it still does.

Letting go of old identities can feel like betrayal. We fear that if we stop being who we were, we might disappoint those who have come to expect that version of us. We wonder if we will still be loved, still be respected, still be worthy if we no longer fit neatly into the box that people have placed us in.

For me, that fear showed up in ways I didn't anticipate. It wasn't just about professional success—it was about the expectations of my community, my family, and even myself. I had been the "Golden Child," the one who always had a plan, the one who led, the one who had it all together. Admitting that I no longer wanted to be defined by that was terrifying.

I remember the first time I said *no* to an opportunity that looked good on paper but didn't align with where I wanted to be. It felt unnatural. It felt selfish. Because for so long, I had been conditioned to believe that my worth was tied to what I *did*—not who I *was*.

But the more I started letting go, the lighter I felt.

Shedding an old identity is not a single act; it is a process. It requires intention, patience, and a willingness to sit in the discomfort of change.

For me, that process included:

> Reevaluating my definitions of success. Was I chasing things because I actually wanted them, or because they were expected of me?
>
> Allowing myself to be vulnerable. Admitting that I didn't have it all figured out, that I didn't always want to be the strong one, that I, too, needed space to grow.
>
> Letting go of relationships that no longer fit. This was one of the hardest parts—realizing that some friendships, some dynamics, and even some professional connections were tied to a version of myself that I was outgrowing.
>
> Sitting with the uncertainty of becoming. Growth isn't always about knowing where you're headed. Sometimes, it's about

trusting that who you are becoming is enough, even if you don't have all the answers yet.

There is something powerful about stepping into yourself fully. About no longer shrinking to fit spaces that weren't built for you. About recognizing that you are allowed to change, to evolve, to redefine yourself on your own terms.

I used to think that shedding old identities meant losing parts of myself. But what I've come to realize is that I'm not losing anything—I'm making room. Room for authenticity. Room for joy. Room for a self-worth that isn't dependent on how much I achieve or how well I fit into the expectations of others.

Shedding is not a loss—it is an arrival. It is the process of unburdening yourself so that you can finally walk freely into the person you were always meant to be.
And for the first time, I am no longer afraid of who that person is becoming

If there's one thing I've learned on this journey, it's that growth does not follow a straight path. It is not a steady climb, nor is it a predictable series of steps that lead to an inevitable moment of enlightenment. Growth is messy. It is full of setbacks, doubts, and moments of questioning everything you thought you knew.

For so long, I believed that healing was a destination. I thought that if I worked hard enough on myself, if I let go of past wounds, if I focused on self-improvement, there would come a day when I'd finally "arrive" at a version of myself that was fully healed, fully whole, and fully at peace. But the truth is, *there is no final version of me.*

Healing is not a finish line. Growth is not a one-time event. Both are ongoing, evolving processes that require constant work, constant grace, and constant self-reflection. There was a time when I thought I had made it.

I had worked through self-doubt. I had confronted my insecurities. I had started shedding old identities, stepping into my authenticity, and prioritizing self-worth over external validation. I was in a better place emotionally, mentally, and spiritually.

And then, one day, I found myself falling back into old habits. I caught myself overworking again, seeking approval in spaces where I swore I didn't need it anymore. I found myself saying *yes* to things that drained me, doubting whether I had really grown at all.

It felt like failure. Like I had undone all the work I had put in. But what I had to remind myself was that growth is not linear. Just because you stumble doesn't mean you haven't grown. Just because old wounds resurface doesn't mean you're back at square one. Just because you have moments of doubt doesn't mean you haven't made progress.

Healing comes in waves. Some days, you feel whole, unstoppable, fully in alignment with who you are becoming. Other days, you feel like you're right back where you started, struggling with the same fears and insecurities you thought you had conquered. But that's the nature of becoming—it is not a straight road, but a winding journey filled with lessons you have to relearn over and over again.

One of the hardest lessons I've had to learn is how to give myself grace. I've always been hard on myself—always holding myself to impossible standards, always pushing myself to do more, to be more, to prove that I am worthy. But growth requires grace. Healing requires patience.

There are days when I fall back into self-doubt. There are moments when I question if I am truly enough. There are times when I feel like I am failing at everything I am working toward. But I remind myself that setbacks are not signs of failure. They are proof that I am still growing. Growth is about learning to be gentle with yourself, to acknowledge that healing is not about perfection—it is about persistence.

Becoming the person you are meant to be is a process of breaking and rebuilding, of unlearning and re-learning, of stepping forward and sometimes stepping back. It is about realizing that you are allowed to change your mind. You are allowed to shift directions. You are allowed to redefine yourself over and over again. There is no set timeline for growth. There is no perfect way to heal. The journey of becoming is full of contradictions:
You can be confident and still have moments of insecurity.
You can know your worth and still seek validation.
You can be strong and still need rest.
You can be healing and still hurt.
And that's okay.

One of the things I've had to learn is how to celebrate progress, even when it feels small. We often wait until we've reached some major milestone before we allow ourselves to feel proud. We wait until we've completely overcome something before we acknowledge how far we've come.

But the truth is, every small step forward is worth celebrating. The moments when you choose yourself. The days when you set a boundary. The times when you recognize your worth, even if only for a second. That is growth. That is healing. That is becoming.

So, I no longer strive for a perfect, linear journey. Instead, I embrace the twists, the turns, the setbacks, and the breakthroughs. Because every step—forward or backward—is a part of who I am becoming. And I am still becoming. Because growth never ends. And that's the beauty of it.

Chapter 8: White

The Guiding Force That Has Kept Me Going

Faith has always been my foundation, the guiding force that has shaped me from childhood to adulthood. It has been my refuge, my source of strength, and at times, my greatest challenge. To understand who I am today, you must understand where my faith journey began. Faith, for many, is a deeply personal experience, but for me, it was always communal. It was something I inherited, something that shaped the very core of my being before I was even old enough to understand it.

I was raised in a household where belief in God was unquestioned, where prayer was not just a ritual but a necessity. But beyond my immediate family, faith was also something that was modeled for me by those who took me under their wing, who nurtured my spirit, and who instilled in me the values that would guide my path.

Faith has been both a gift and a burden. A gift because it has been my anchor in life's storms, my compass in times of uncertainty. A burden because, at times, it has felt like a weight too heavy to carry, filled with expectations that often felt impossible to meet. The journey of faith is rarely linear, and mine has been no exception. It has been filled with moments of deep conviction and moments of profound doubt. It has lifted me up and, at times, made me question everything I thought I knew.

But through it all, faith has remained. It has evolved, shifted, and expanded, but it has never left me. This chapter is about that journey—the moments of clarity, the struggles, the revelations, and ultimately, the freedom I found in embracing faith on my own terms.

My faith journey did not start with my parents or even my church. It began in an unexpected place—a home daycare run by a deeply spiritual couple, one of whom was a pastor of a local *Holiness Church*. My parents, though believers, had not yet fully immersed themselves in the faith at that time. When they were searching for childcare, they found this couple who would later become my godparents. From the age of three well into my teenage years, they were a foundational guiding force in my spiritual life, shaping not only my beliefs but also my understanding of what it meant to walk with God.

My godparents lived and breathed their faith. Their home was a place where holiness was not just preached, but practiced in every aspect of life. From the moment you stepped inside, there was a sense of sacredness—prayer before meals, scriptures quoted in casual conversations, and gospel music humming softly in the background. They instilled in me the principles of salvation, righteousness, and a life dedicated to honoring God. Their commitment was unwavering, their devotion evident in everything they did.

To them, faith was more than attending church on Sundays—it was a daily, intentional walk with God. Every trial was met with prayer, every decision weighed against biblical teachings, and every victory credited to divine grace. They ensured I knew the power of fasting, the importance of scripture, and the necessity of living a life that aligned with holiness. Their love was evident in their guidance, their correction, and the time they spent nurturing my spiritual growth.

One thing I never doubted was their love for me. I never feared that their love would waver. They had dedicated themselves to shaping me into a man of faith. It was through their teachings that I first encountered God in a deep, personal way. It was in their home that I first learned what it meant to believe, to trust, and to walk in faith. Their love was constant, and their faith was the foundation upon which my own spiritual journey was built.

As a child, I often attended church services with them, sometimes as many as three or four times a week. I can still remember those church services. The fervent prayers, the shouting, the deep, raw worship—it all ignited something in me. I loved church. The *Holiness Church,* the Pentecostal church, felt like home. It was home. It was electric, filled with passion and a deep sense of spiritual connection. It was in those moments, watching the saints rejoice and seeing faith come alive, that I knew Pentecostalism was where I belonged.

Growing up in Pentecostalism, however, meant growing up with a very rigid framework of what it meant to be holy and what it meant to be saved. There were rules, both spoken and unspoken—rules that governed how you dressed, who you associated with, how you spoke, and how you lived. There was a deep-seated belief that holiness was the only way, that any deviation from our teachings was a step toward damnation. We were conditioned to believe that our way was the only way, and this created an inherent judgment toward those who did not live as we did. We were trained to associate only with each other, to avoid outside influences, and to uphold impossible standards. If our leaders said it, we did it. And because of that, there was a certain level of trauma embedded within our faith.

Growing up in Pentecostalism, I had been taught about the necessity of receiving the Holy Ghost from an early age. It was not enough to simply believe in God—you had to be *filled* with His spirit. This was the expectation for all who truly sought holiness. It wasn't optional—it was essential.

For Pentecostals, this experience is not just another step in one's spiritual walk—it is the pinnacle of divine connection, the moment when God Himself fills you with His power. It is the moment when the presence of God becomes undeniable, when the weight of His spirit overtakes you completely. It is a rite of passage, a seal of righteousness, a sign that you are truly walking in the fullness of God's will.

For years, I had watched others *tarry* at the altar, crying out to God, calling on the name of Jesus repeatedly, hoping and believing that at any moment, the Spirit would fall. Tarrying was an intense, emotional experience. It was not a quiet, solemn prayer; it was an act of complete surrender. It meant kneeling for hours, hands lifted, voice straining as you called on Jesus over and over again, sometimes until your throat felt raw. It meant tears streaming down your face, sweat pouring from your body, as the saints gathered around you, rocking with intercession, urging you to "press through." Some would say, "Call Him like you need Him!" Others would say, "You're almost there!" But only God decided when the moment would come. And when it did, it was unmistakable.

On a Sunday night in May, at the age of sixteen, I had a defining moment in my faith. It was the night I received the baptism of the Holy Ghost. On that night, as I engaged in fervent prayer, my mother alongside me, I felt that moment rush over me like a mighty wind.

That night, as I tarried, I felt something shift inside of me. The weight of my own voice faded, replaced by something unfamiliar yet deeply known. The words pouring from my mouth were not my own, and yet, they belonged to me. My entire body felt electrified, consumed by something greater than myself. And at that moment, I knew that I had received what they had been praying over me for years. I had finally been filled.

I will never forget the overwhelming joy I felt. It was a joy that was not rooted in accomplishment but in divine connection. I was proud to finally say the phrase I had heard the elders echo my entire life: *"I'm saved, sanctified, baptized, and filled with the precious gift of the Holy Ghost!"* It felt like validation—not just from God, but from the church, from my spiritual community. I had been marked. I had been chosen.

That moment solidified my faith. It was more than just a religious milestone—it was the evidence that I was walking in the will of God. But with that validation came expectations. Suddenly, I was no longer just a church member—I was someone who had been *filled*, someone who had been called to a higher standard. I wanted to be seen as holy, as righteous, as one of the faithful.

I wanted to be everything that God had called me to be. I wanted to be everything the church had prepared me to be. But there were parts of me I wasn't sure could ever fully belong—things unspoken, lingering beneath the surface. I had been filled with the Spirit, yet I carried the weight of things I couldn't name. And I often wondered if they were meant to be overcome or simply accepted.

Just two months after being filled, I received my calling to preach. I can still remember the weight of that moment—the gravity of what it meant to be called into ministry at just sixteen years old. The call was not a whisper, not a fleeting thought, but an undeniable pull on my spirit. I felt it in the stillness of prayer, in the echoes of scripture, in the way my heart stirred when I stood behind a pulpit for the first time.

Two years later, I was ordained as an Elder in the church, a title that carried immense responsibility. While my peers were preparing for college, prom, and the milestones of typical teenage years, I was preparing sermons, studying theology, and seeking to understand the depths of God's word.

Being a young minister meant stepping into rooms where I was often the youngest, where experience was measured in decades, and where wisdom was expected to be earned through time and trial. Yet, I was entrusted with a calling that did not wait for age or seniority. I was expected to lead, to counsel, to uplift—to be a pillar in the very community that had shaped me. The pulpit became my home, the Word my refuge. There was nothing quite like the fire that surged through me when I preached, the way the words flowed as if they were not my own, but divinely given.

But with that anointing came a deep and unspoken pressure—the pressure to live righteously, to walk upright, to be above reproach. There was little room for error, little space for humanity. I was seen as a spiritual leader, a guide, a vessel. People came to me for advice, for prayer, for answers. And while I loved walking in my calling, I was also still just a teenager, trying to navigate my own identity and my own understanding of who I was.

I had fully embraced my calling, but I had not fully embraced myself. I was a young Black man, a leader in my church, and deeply devoted to my faith—yet there were parts of me I was still trying to reconcile. In the world I had grown up in, some things could not coexist. The church taught that certain truths were meant to be prayed away, that difference had no place in the pulpit, no place in the kingdom. And so, I was left wondering—where did that leave me?

The weight of this internal conflict was immense. I felt as if I were always wearing a mask—speaking of God's love while quietly wondering if that love truly saw all of me. For many, the church was a place of refuge, yet it was also a place where some feared they might never be fully known. One could preach about grace, about forgiveness, about God's boundless love—but speaking too much of oneself felt like a risk too great to take.

For years, I prayed. I fasted, I tarried, I sought answers. I asked God to help me, to take away the questions that lingered in the quiet moments. I threw myself into ministry, believing that if I preached hard enough, prayed fervently enough, surrendered completely enough, maybe—just maybe—God would give me peace.

I grew up in an environment where faith was absolute, unquestionable, and the foundation of everything. The sermons were filled with fire, conviction, and an unwavering stance on what was considered righteous and what was not. I remember sitting in the pews, listening to pastors preach about the wrath of God, about the dangers of straying from His will. The message was clear: holiness was the only acceptable path, and anything outside of that was a deviation from His plan. And so, I learned to guard certain parts of myself, to push them aside, to present only what I thought would keep me in His favor.

I remember countless altar calls where I would cry out, searching for a breakthrough, for an answer. If faith could move mountains, why did I still feel the weight of what I carried? I listened as others testified about their own deliverance, how they had been "set free" from the things the church told them they had to leave behind. I wanted to say the same—to stand before the congregation and declare that God had done a work in me. But no matter how much I prayed, no matter how hard I tried, I was still me.

The tension between my faith and the expectations placed upon me felt like a weight I couldn't shake. For years, I wrestled with questions I was too afraid to voice. I had been taught that holiness required separation, that righteousness meant conforming to a standard I wasn't sure I could meet. But then, a thought took root—one that refused to leave me: *Why would God call me, knowing exactly who I was, if I was never meant to belong? Was I meant to spend my life at odds with myself in order to follow Him?*

That question unraveled everything I had believed about myself. It forced me to consider the possibility that—just maybe—God had called me as I was, not as I was trying to become. Maybe my being wasn't a failing or a fault, not something to be corrected, but something intentionally woven into my existence, designed with purpose.

That realization did not come easily. It took years of unlearning, of letting go of shame, of embracing grace in a way I had never been taught. But when it came, it set me free. I am still called. I am still anointed. And I am still wholly loved by God. That, more than anything, is the sermon I needed to hear. And today, it is the sermon I live.

The Black church has long been a sanctuary—a place where we, as a people, have found refuge from the oppression of the outside world. It has been the epicenter of civil rights movements, a place of empowerment, and a source of community. Yet, for some, that same sacred space can also feel like a place of distance, where belonging is not always guaranteed, and unspoken lines dictate who is fully embraced.

The paradox of the Black church is that it has historically been a place of both liberation and oppression. It has been the place where Black people have found freedom from systemic injustice, yet it is also the place where many of us have been shackled by doctrine. It is a place that preaches unconditional love, yet imposes conditions on who is worthy to receive it.

The Black church is complex. It is both a place of healing and a place of hurt, a source of strength yet, at times, a space of judgment. It is where faith and belonging can feel at odds, where questions arise that are not easily answered. And for a long time, I wrestled with that tension. I wanted to worship freely, to stand boldly in my faith without questioning whether I truly belonged. But belonging, I realized, often came with conditions. It meant quieting certain thoughts, tempering my voice, and conforming to expectations that left little room for authenticity.

There were moments when I would sit in church and feel the weight of messages that weren't directed at me, yet still felt deeply personal. The call to "pray away" sin, the warnings about the dangers of living in the flesh—it all reinforced the idea that something within me was at odds with God's grace. And so, I fought. I prayed, I fasted, I sought renewal, believing that if I could just be *good enough*, the weight I carried would be lifted. But in time, I came to understand: the burden was never mine to bear. It was not something within me that needed to be changed—it was the shame I had been taught to carry, the belief that I had to prove myself worthy of love. Worthy of God's love.

Over time, I realized that my faith could not be dictated by the expectations of others. That the God I knew—the God who had carried me through life's most difficult moments—was not a God of condemnation, but of love. I had to deconstruct the messages I had internalized, to sift through what was truly divine and what was simply human interpretation. I had to find my own way, my own understanding of what it meant to be Bryson. And in that journey, I found freedom.

Faith, at its core, is not about exclusion. It is about embracing the fullness of who we are and recognizing that we were never meant to be anything other than exactly who we were created to be. God was never concerned with my denomination or church affiliation. He was not bound by the opinions of others. He was concerned with me—my heart, the way I loved others, and how I honored Him in my daily life.

For years, I had been taught that faith was about meeting a set of expectations—rules that dictated what holiness looked like, how righteousness should be performed, and what it meant to be "right" in God's eyes. But faith was never meant to be a rigid set of checkboxes. Faith was about connection, relationship, and an ever-evolving journey toward love and truth.

Letting go of the need to perform for God was not easy. It took years of unlearning, years of allowing myself to reimagine what faith could look like outside of the traditions I had been raised in. There were nights when I wrestled with guilt, when I questioned if I was straying too far from the foundation that had been built for me. But then I would remember: God had been present in every part of my journey, even in my moments of doubt. He had never left me, even when I had questioned Him. If God had been patient with me, why couldn't I be patient with myself?

Faith is not about performance; it is about relationship. And today, I stand firm in the truth that I am fully known and wholly loved. My faith is not measured by how well I conform, nor are my prayers unheard because I do not meet expectations set by others. I am just as much a child of God now as I was when I tarried at the altar, crying out for the Holy Ghost. God did not love me more then, nor does He love me any less now. And in that truth, I found peace.

I no longer believe that faith is about rigid rules or exclusionary practices. Faith, at its core, is about love—real, unconditional love. It is about grace. It is about truth. It is about allowing myself to be seen, not only by God but by myself. For the first time in my life, I feel free in my faith, knowing that God's love for me is not dependent on my ability to meet human-imposed expectations. It is not dependent on my ability to adhere to a doctrine that leaves little room for grace. God's love is constant. God's love is vast. And God's love is for me. This is faith. This is freedom. This is truth.

For years, my faith was something I carried like a weight—something that dictated how I moved, how I spoke, and even how I saw myself. It was the framework through which I viewed the world, but it was also the structure that kept me bound. I spent so much time trying to fit into the narrow mold that had been set for me, believing that holiness meant denying parts of myself that I could never erase. But true faith is not about restriction—it is about liberation. It took me years to unlearn the belief that my worthiness in God's eyes depended on my ability to conform. The more I grew, the more I realized that faith should be a refuge, not a prison.

I no longer see myself as a contradiction. I am Bryson, and my faith remains unwavering. These truths are not in conflict—they coexist within me. The love I feel from God is not conditional, and I do not have to fight for a seat at the table of grace. While the church may have wrestled with making space for those who did not fit its mold, God never did. In that understanding, I have freed myself from the weight of shame and guilt. My faith now brings me peace, not turmoil.

My journey has been one of deconstruction and reconstruction—of breaking down the beliefs that were rooted in fear and rebuilding a faith centered in love. I have come to understand that faith is deeply personal. It is not about rules, denominations, or proving one's righteousness. It is about connection—about living in a way that honors both God and the person He created me to be. The closer I got to God, the less concerned I became with the approval of people. It is a journey that continues every day, one that requires grace, patience, and a willingness to embrace the unknown.

And so, I move forward, no longer bound by fear but propelled by faith. I walk this Earth knowing that my existence is purposeful, my voice is valuable, and my faith is unshakable. I am still growing, still evolving, still deepening my understanding of what it means to live a life of faith. But one thing is certain—I am enough, just as I am. And for the first time, I can say that with absolute conviction.

Chapter 9: Orange

How I've Expressed Myself in a World That Often Tried to Silence Me

For much of my life, I never considered myself creative. The word itself seemed reserved for people who could paint vivid portraits, compose beautiful music, or design something breathtaking from scratch. I admired those who could take an empty space and fill it with something original, something that had never existed before. I saw creativity as something external, something I could observe in others but never truly embody myself.

I was always the structured, high-achieving, goal-oriented person who thrived in environments where success was measurable. I knew how to check the right boxes, follow the path laid before me, and produce results. But creativity? That felt different. It felt abstract, fluid, something you couldn't quantify. And because I didn't see myself painting, sculpting, or playing an instrument, I assumed that creativity was simply something I didn't possess.

But over time, I began to understand that creativity is not just about what you produce—it is about how you see the world. It is about the way you piece things together, the way you interpret and interact with life. It's about finding new solutions, reimagining old ideas, and making space for something different. And looking back, I now realize that creativity had always been with me. I just hadn't recognized it.

I saw it in the way I navigated expectations, in the way I adapted to different environments, in the way I found ways to express myself when words alone weren't enough. Creativity wasn't just in art—it was in the ability to find new ways to exist in a world that often tried to confine me. I had spent so much time assuming I wasn't creative that I failed to see the ways I had been shaping, molding, and creating a version of myself that was uniquely my own all along.

This realization didn't happen overnight. It came in pieces, moments of clarity scattered throughout my life—moments when I saw the way I naturally gravitated toward storytelling, problem-solving, reimagining spaces, and shaping experiences for myself and others. Creativity had been there, just waiting for me to acknowledge it. And once I did, I was able to embrace it fully—not just as something I admired in others, but as something that had always been a part of me.

Before I ever saw myself as creative, I was unknowingly engaging in acts of creativity every single day. As a child, I was drawn to storytelling, organizing, structuring, and bringing ideas to life, but I didn't recognize those things as "creative" because they didn't fit into the traditional mold of artistry that I had been taught to admire. I thought creativity belonged to those who could paint murals or play an instrument effortlessly, and because I couldn't, I assumed I wasn't one of them.

But when I reflect on my childhood, I now see creativity in the way I told stories, the way I planned events, and the way I could piece together thoughts in a way that made people stop and listen. I see it in the way I could look at a situation and imagine all the ways it could be different, all the ways it could be better. I see it in the moments when I would take ordinary things and turn them into something meaningful—not necessarily with my hands, but with my mind.

There were moments, small and fleeting, when my creativity tried to introduce itself to me. When I wrote elaborate stories in my notebooks. When I restructured school projects so they had more impact. When I envisioned better systems, better ways of communicating, better ways of doing things. At the time, I thought I was just being efficient or strategic, but now I realize—I was creating. I was building something out of nothing. And that, in itself, is an act of artistry.

It took me years to realize that creativity isn't just about making something that can be framed or performed. It's about bringing something new into existence. It's about reimagining possibilities and making connections that weren't obvious before. And while I may not have seen it at the time, creativity had always been embedded in who I was. It was not something I had to learn—it was something I had to recognize.

Growing up, I was raised in a world that valued structure, discipline, and excellence. Success was defined by tangible achievements—academic performance, leadership roles, being someone that others could be proud of. Creativity, on the other hand, was often seen as secondary. It was appreciated, but only when it fit within certain boundaries—public speaking, ministry, or leadership development. Anything outside of that wasn't discouraged, but it wasn't necessarily nurtured either.

This shaped how I viewed myself. I excelled at what I was supposed to excel at, focusing on the things that were encouraged and praised. I pushed myself to meet every expectation, to prove that I was serious, hardworking, and responsible. But in doing so, I neglected the parts of me that wanted to explore freely, to create just for the sake of creating.

I spent years believing that creativity was indulgent, something that distracted from "real" success. I thought that investing in creativity meant taking away from more important things—until I realized that my ability to think differently, to see possibilities where others didn't, and to express myself in ways that were uniquely my own was my greatest strength.

It wasn't just about writing or creating something physical—it was about shaping my own identity in a world that often tried to define it for me. For the longest time, I thought of creativity as something external—something separate from my personal growth. But as I grew older, I realized that creativity wasn't just about expression—it was about survival.

When I struggled with self-doubt, I wrote my way through it. When I felt out of place in certain spaces, I created my own. When I felt the weight of expectations press down on me, I used creativity to carve out breathing room.

Creativity became my safe space, a place where I could explore who I was without judgment. I used it to process emotions that felt too complicated to untangle otherwise. It allowed me to redefine myself, to find new ways to exist in a world that often felt restrictive. I learned that creativity is a form of resilience. It is the ability to see beyond the present, to imagine something different, something better. It is what allows us to create a vision for our lives beyond what we've been told is possible.

For years, I measured success by external validation. It was about achieving goals that others could recognize and respect—titles, recognition, positions of influence. I thought success meant proving myself, earning the approval of those who had set the standards before me.

But as I embraced creativity, I started to realize that success is not about meeting expectations—it is about creating meaning.

Success isn't about how others define it. It's about what makes you feel fulfilled, what makes you feel whole. It's about creating something for yourself, on your own terms.

I no longer chase validation. I create my own sense of achievement. I no longer feel the need to fit into a mold—I am shaping my own. And in doing so, I have found something even greater than success: freedom.

I once thought creativity was something I lacked. Now, I see that it has been with me all along. It was in the way I navigated expectations, in the way I built spaces where I could be myself, in the way I transformed challenges into opportunities.

Creativity is not just about art. It is about the courage to express yourself in a world that often tries to silence you. It is about seeing beyond what is in front of you and daring to imagine something new. It is about taking ownership of your story, your identity, and your voice.

For anyone who has ever doubted their creativity, know this: Creativity is not about talent. It is not about being the best at something. It is about showing up as yourself, unapologetically, and creating a space for your truth. That is what I have learned. That is what I will continue to do. Because in the end, creativity is not just about what you make—it is about who you become in the process.

Chapter 10: Purple

The Lessons I've Learned Along the Way

Wisdom is not something you wake up with one day. It's not a medal you receive or a title you earn after a certain number of years. Instead, it's something you gain in the quiet moments—through mistakes, through victories, through heartbreak, and through healing. It's the voice inside that reminds you of everything you've survived and everything you're capable of becoming.

I never thought of myself as someone with wisdom to share until I wrote *Whispers of Wisdom*, my first published book. At the time, I wasn't sure if I had anything worth saying, let alone anything people would actually listen to. But as I reflected on my life, I realized that wisdom isn't about having all the answers—it's about asking the right questions. It's about the lessons that shape you, the truths that challenge you, and the growth that transforms you.

When I first held *Whispers of Wisdom* in my hands, I felt the weight of my own journey in its pages. It was filled with reflections on resilience, on faith, on self-worth, and on the power of learning from life itself. It was a reminder that wisdom is not something we acquire alone—it's something we pass down, something we share, something we build together.

Purple, to me, has always symbolized wisdom. It is the color of depth, of reflection, of experience. And in this chapter, I want to explore the lessons that have shaped me—not as a final list of truths, but as guiding lights that continue to lead me forward.

Lesson One: You Are Not Defined by Your Mistakes

For a long time, I struggled with the weight of perfectionism. I believed that my worth was directly tied to my ability to succeed—to always get it right, to never make mistakes, to be someone that others could look up to. But life has a way of humbling you, of showing you that failure is not just inevitable but necessary.

One of the hardest lessons I had to learn was that mistakes do not define me. They do not erase my worth or diminish my value. Instead, they are the very things that sharpen my character, refine my purpose, and teach me resilience.

There were moments in my life when I let guilt consume me, when I replayed past missteps over and over again, convinced that they made me unworthy of grace. But wisdom has taught me that redemption is not just possible—it is a part of the journey.

The truth is, failure is only failure if you refuse to learn from it. Every mistake, every misstep, every setback is an opportunity to grow, to refine, to become better. And once I realized that, I stopped fearing failure and started embracing it as part of the process.

Lesson Two: Healing Is Not Linear

When I first began my journey of healing—whether it was from childhood wounds, internalized shame, or the pressures of constantly proving myself—I thought it would be a straight path. I believed that if I just did the work, if I just pushed forward, I would eventually reach a place of wholeness where the pain no longer touched me.

But healing is not a straight road. It is a winding path with detours, setbacks, and days when you feel like you're back at the very beginning. There were times when I thought I had moved past certain wounds, only for them to resurface in unexpected ways. There were moments when I felt strong, only to break down when I least expected it.

I used to see this as failure, as evidence that I wasn't truly healing. But wisdom has shown me that healing is not about arriving at a perfect state of peace—it's about allowing yourself grace in the process.

Real healing means learning to sit with discomfort, to acknowledge the parts of yourself that still need work, and to understand that progress is not measured by how quickly you move forward but by your willingness to keep going.

Lesson Three: Checking Boxes Is Not Success

For much of my life, I believed that success was a checklist. Graduate high school with honors? Check. Get multiple degrees? Check. Land leadership roles? Check. Win awards? Check. Each milestone felt like another box to be marked, another external validation of my worth. I convinced myself that if I just kept checking these boxes, I would eventually reach a point where I felt fulfilled, whole, and at peace.

But as I climbed higher and achieved more, I started to realize something unsettling—*success does not guarantee happiness*. Each time I completed a major milestone, there was always another one waiting for me. The list never ended. Instead of feeling accomplished, I felt trapped in an endless cycle of doing, achieving, and proving. It wasn't enough to succeed; I had to keep succeeding.

I had been conditioned to believe that success was about meeting expectations—societal expectations, family expectations, professional expectations. But checking boxes is about *meeting standards set by others*, not necessarily about fulfillment, joy, or alignment with one's true purpose. And when your life becomes about meeting expectations instead of creating meaning, success feels empty.

There were times when I reached a goal I had worked tirelessly for, only to feel absolutely nothing once I got there. The awards, the titles, the external recognition—none of it filled the spaces in me that longed for something deeper. I had to learn that *checking boxes is not the same as living with purpose.*

True success isn't about constantly moving to the next milestone. It's about finding fulfillment in the journey. It's about creating a life that feels meaningful beyond the accolades. It's about defining success for yourself, not through the lens of others.

Once I shifted my mindset, I started asking myself new questions:

Am I actually happy with the life I'm building?

Does this achievement bring me joy, or am I doing it because it's what I think I'm supposed to do?

Who am I outside of my accomplishments?

The biggest lesson I've learned is that success is not a destination—it's a way of being. It's living a life that feels honest, aligned, and fulfilling. It's about *impact*, not just achievement. It's about *purpose*, not just productivity. And it's about choosing to create a life that nourishes your soul, not just one that looks good on paper.

Now, I no longer measure my life by how many boxes I can check. I measure it by the depth of my experiences, the authenticity of my relationships, and the peace I feel when I wake up each morning. Because at the end of the day, *checking boxes will never be enough if your life is missing meaning.*

Lesson Four: You Get to Define Yourself

For so much of my life, I allowed others to define me. I was the high achiever, the responsible one, the leader, the one who always had it together. I was the student who made his family proud, the professional who exceeded expectations, the person who worked tirelessly to be seen as *enough*. Without realizing it, I had spent years shaping my identity around what others expected of me.

It wasn't until I started to question those expectations that I realized how much of myself I had been suppressing. The world had given me labels, but I had never taken the time to define myself on my own terms. Who was I beyond the roles I had been assigned? Beyond the accomplishments? Beyond the carefully curated version of myself that I presented to the world?

The truth is, no one else gets to tell you who you are. Not society, not your family, not your mentors, not your job. People will always have opinions about what you should do, how you should behave, and who you should be—but the most important voice in that conversation is your own.

I had to learn that defining myself meant letting go of the need for external approval. It meant understanding that I was not obligated to fit into any single mold. I did not have to conform to the version of myself that was the most acceptable, the most palatable, the most easy to digest. I could be complex. I could be evolving. I could be *whole* on my own terms.

This realization was both liberating and terrifying. When you've spent your whole life being who others need you to be, stepping into your own truth can feel like a betrayal. But in reality, it's the most necessary form of self-love. Defining yourself means honoring the fullness of your being, embracing your contradictions, and allowing yourself the space to grow without restriction.

Now, I no longer live for the approval of others. I don't ask for permission to be myself. I don't shrink or contort myself to fit into expectations that no longer serve me. I am constantly evolving, constantly learning, constantly stepping into a deeper understanding of who I am—and that journey is mine to own.

You get to define yourself. You get to take up space. You get to rewrite the narratives that others have placed on you. And once you realize that, you become unstoppable.

Lesson Five: I Don't Know Everything

The moment I realized I didn't have to know everything was the moment I found freedom. For years, I thought wisdom meant always having an answer, always being sure, always knowing what came next. But the truth is, some of the wisest people I've met are the ones who aren't afraid to admit they don't know.

Life is a continuous journey of learning, of being open to new perspectives, of allowing yourself to evolve. I've learned that there is strength in saying, *I don't know, but I'm willing to learn.* There is power in admitting that you are still growing.

Wisdom is not about certainty—it's about curiosity. And the moment you think you've figured it all out is the moment you stop growing.

Lesson Six: The Right People Will See You

For a long time, I exhausted myself trying to prove my worth to people who were never going to see me for who I truly was. I would overextend myself, work twice as hard, and constantly seek validation from those who either couldn't or wouldn't give it. I thought that if I just showed up in the right way, said the right things, and played by the right rules, I would finally be accepted.

But wisdom has taught me a profound truth: *The right people will see you, and you won't have to shrink, bend, or prove yourself for them to do so.*

There were times in my life when I felt invisible in rooms where I should have belonged. I was overlooked, underestimated, and sometimes even dismissed altogether. At first, I thought this was a reflection of me—that maybe I wasn't good enough, that I needed to work harder. But I later realized that some people are simply incapable of recognizing the value you bring, and that has nothing to do with you and everything to do with them.

The right people—the ones meant to be in your life, in your circle, in your corner—will see you. They will recognize your worth without you having to prove it. They will celebrate you without conditions. They will uplift you without expectations. These are the people who will help you grow, who will challenge you to become better, and who will remind you that you were never invisible to begin with.

Once I stopped trying to force belonging in places that weren't meant for me, I found peace. I learned to walk away from spaces that drained me, from people who required me to prove my worth over and over again. I started seeking relationships, friendships, and communities that felt aligned, that made me feel seen, valued, and appreciated.

And when I did, everything changed. Because the truth is, *when you stop chasing validation from the wrong people, you make room for the right ones to enter your life.*

If there's one thing I've learned, it's that wisdom is not about arriving at a final, absolute truth—it's about staying open to the lessons life continues to teach. Every chapter of my life has come with new revelations, new struggles, and new opportunities to grow.

Wisdom is not a destination, nor is it something you simply acquire with age or experience. It is a process—one that requires reflection, humility, and the courage to evolve. It's the ability to look back with gratitude for the lessons learned and to look forward with curiosity about what's still ahead.

The lessons I've shared in this chapter are not just reflections of the past; they are tools I carry with me as I continue to build the life I want. They are the reminders that mistakes do not define me, that growth is never linear, and that true wisdom comes not from having all the answers, but from knowing which questions to ask.

So, as I step into the next phase of my journey, I do so with a heart that is open, a mind that is willing to grow, and a soul that is at peace with the fact that I will never know everything. And maybe that's the wisest thing of all.

Chapter 11: Brown

The Grounding Forces in My Life

I have always believed that who we are is not just shaped by what we do, but by who loves us, who supports us, and who stands beside us. No matter how much I have achieved, how far I have gone, or how much I have grown, I would be nothing without the love that has carried me.

There is a kind of love that grounds you, that holds you steady even when life shakes you. It is the kind of love that doesn't demand anything in return, that simply exists—deep, unwavering, and unconditional. It is the love of a mother who sees the full picture of who you are before you even understand it yourself. The love of a grandmother who in her eyes, you can do no wrong. The love of the people who have poured into you, who have prayed over you, who have made sure that you always knew, no matter what, you were never alone.

This chapter is about that love. About the relationships that have made me who I am. About the grounding forces in my life that have given me a place to return to, no matter how far I've traveled. Because at the end of the day, no matter how high you climb, no matter how much you achieve, what truly matters is knowing that you are loved.

If I could name the single greatest source of grounding in my life, it would be my mother. My mother has been my anchor, my protector, my first teacher in what it means to love without limits. She has always been the kind of person who makes sacrifices without hesitation, who carries more than her fair share of burdens so that those she loves can walk a little lighter. She gave and gave—not just in material ways but in emotional, spiritual, and deeply personal ways.

Her love was not just spoken; it was shown in the way she lived. She worked tirelessly to provide, often putting her own wants and needs on hold so that I could have everything I needed. I saw her strength in the late nights, the early mornings, the way she stretched every dollar, and the way she always found a way—even when it seemed like there was no way. She made miracles out of the mundane.

If there is one thing I have always known about my mother, it is this—she always had an answer. No matter what the situation was, no matter what challenges arose, she carried herself with a confidence and certainty that made me feel like there was no problem too big for her to solve. She was steady, she was sure, and she always made things work.

Growing up, I never wanted for anything. My mother made sure of that. It wasn't just about material things—it was about security, about stability, about knowing that no matter what happened, she would always find a way. There was no chaos in her presence, no moments where I ever had to wonder whether things would be okay. Because with her, they always were.

She had a way of making life feel seamless. When something needed to be done, she did it. When I had a problem, she had a solution. When I doubted myself, she was there to remind me exactly who I was. She never let uncertainty touch me, never let me feel like I had to figure things out on my own. She was always there with an answer, a plan, and the assurance that everything was already taken care of.

I can remember countless moments when I would come to her with something that felt like a crisis—a difficult decision, a problem I couldn't untangle, a moment where I felt lost in my own uncertainty. And every time, she would listen patiently, nodding as I poured out my worries. Then, when I was done, she would simply say, "Well, here's what we're going to do." And just like that, the weight would lift.

Her confidence became my confidence. Her ability to navigate life with such clarity taught me that there is always a way forward. She never allowed me to sit in uncertainty for too long. Not because she rushed me, but because she wanted me to understand that no problem was too big, no situation too uncertain, no challenge too impossible.
Even in the times when I felt unsure of myself, she never was. She believed in me before I ever learned to believe in myself. She saw things in me that I hadn't yet discovered. And because she saw them, she made sure that I did, too.

One of the greatest gifts she ever gave me was the ability to trust in my own wisdom, to know that even when life felt uncertain, I had everything I needed within me. That kind of assurance, that kind of unwavering support. That is the foundation that has carried me through every season of my life.

Beyond her sacrifices, her faith was a beacon of light in my life. My mother prayed over me. She spoke life into me before I ever understood what that meant. I remember waking up in the middle of the night as a child and hearing her whispering prayers, covering our home, speaking blessings over my future. During her times of encouragement, she would always remind me: "You must always remain thankful. You must always stay prayerful. And most of all, you've got to be saved." She carried a belief so strong that, even in the hardest of times, she never let me see her doubt. Instead, she let me see her faith.

And no matter what, she always made sure I knew I was enough. I remember one night, in my early teenage years, when I came home after a particularly rough day. I had been carrying the weight of so many expectations—expectations from school, from church, from the world around me that demanded so much of me. I sat down at the kitchen table, exhausted, and she could see it all over me.

She didn't pry. She didn't push me to talk before I was ready. Instead, she simply placed a plate of food in front of me, sat down, and said, "You don't have to prove anything to anyone. You are already everything you need to be." That moment has stayed with me my entire life.

Her love was never transactional. It was never based on what I accomplished, never given only when I met certain expectations. It was steady, constant, unwavering. And that kind of love? That is what keeps a person grounded.

She has always been my greatest source of strength, faith, and unconditional love. And if there is one thing I carry from her, it is this: To love deeply, to believe in people fully, and to never let the world tell me that I am not enough.

If love had a sound, it would be my paternal grandmother's laughter—full, rich, and unapologetic. The kind of laugh that fills a room, that makes people turn their heads and smile, that reminds you that joy doesn't have to be quiet to be beautiful.

If safety had a form, it would be her arms, always open, always welcoming, always home. No matter what was happening in my world—whether I was feeling lost, misunderstood, or even just exhausted—her embrace had a way of making it all feel lighter.

If faith had a rhythm, it would be the way her feet moved across the kitchen floor, shouting and dancing beside me, lost in the spirit, but somehow always aware of me. She was a woman of deep conviction, but more than that, she was a woman of deep love.

My grandmother has always been my safe place. There is nowhere in this world I have ever felt more secure, more seen, more celebrated, than in her presence. In her eyes, I could do no wrong. Not because she was blind to my flaws, but because her love for me was unconditional.

She has this rare ability to make everyone around her feel like they matter, like they are important. But with me? I was special. I was her heart, her baby, the one she would go to war for. There was never a doubt in my mind that she loved me, and she never let me forget it.

She knew when to comfort, when to push, when to protect, and when to just let me be. No matter what life threw at me, she was always the one waiting on the sidelines, ready to step in, ready to catch me when I fell—sometimes quite literally.

I'll never forget third grade, the year I embarrassed myself in the school-wide spelling bee. I was ready. I had practiced. I was confident. But the first word I got—"Saturday"—tripped me up in the worst way. I spelled it with a "d" instead of a "t," and just like that, I was out. First round. I could feel my face burning as I walked back to my seat, my confidence shattered.

It wasn't just about the mistake—it was about how many people had been watching. It was about expectations. My teachers, my classmates, my family—I didn't want to disappoint anyone. I sat there, head down, barely listening as the competition continued without me.

But my grandmother? She didn't let me sit in that embarrassment for long.

She checked me out of school. She walked right up to the front office, signed me out, and we left. And instead of spending the rest of the day feeling sorry for myself, we turned it into something else. We went to lunch, just the two of us, and by the time the meal was over, I had all but forgotten the spelling bee.

To her, it wasn't about whether I won or lost—it was about making sure I knew that one moment didn't define me. That I was still smart, still capable, still worthy, even when I messed up. That's who she has always been.

She was also my greatest escape artist. Growing up, I was never great at sports, but I somehow ended up playing little league football. I hated it. Absolutely hated it. But my dad? He was my coach, and quitting wasn't an option.

I tried to stick it out. I really did. But every practice, every game, I felt like I was just pretending to enjoy it. I wasn't built for the aggression or the drills that made my legs ache. But I kept showing up, week after week, because that's what was expected of me. Until one day, I'd had enough.

Right there in the middle of a game, I ran straight off the field. Past my team, past my dad, past all the other parents in the stands. I ran straight into Granny's arms. She didn't hesitate—she took my hand, and we left. Just like that.

We went on to do our own thing, leaving football behind as just another passing childhood phase. She never forced me to stick it out, never made me feel bad for wanting to walk away. She just let me be myself. And that was the magic of her love.

There are people in this world who love you because they are supposed to. And then there are people who love you because they choose to, again and again, every single day. That's my grandmother. She is my laughter on the hardest days, my voice of wisdom in uncertain times, my proof that love can be steady, unwavering, and fierce. She has always been the light in my darkest moments, my biggest fan, my safe place. To know her love is to know what it means to be truly cherished. And for that, I am endlessly grateful.

Not every grounding force in life comes from blood. Some of the most transformative relationships in my life have been with the people who chose me, and whom I chose in return. Family, in its truest form, is not just about shared genetics—it's about shared experiences, shared burdens, and shared love.

I have been blessed with friends who feel like family, people who have walked beside me in some of my highest and lowest moments, people who have seen me, affirmed me, and held space for me in ways I never knew I needed. These are the people who didn't just witness my journey—they actively shaped it.

Some of these friendships began in childhood, others in college, and some through shared experiences in adulthood. My fraternity brothers, who became more than just peers, became my anchors, my confidants, my brothers in every sense of the word. The late-night conversations, the moments of encouragement before major life changes, the simple reminders that I was never alone and *"wasn't heavy"*—all of these were acts of love that helped me become who I am today.

There is something sacred about finding people who truly see you. Not just the version of you that is polished, prepared, and socially acceptable—but the version of you that is flawed, uncertain, and still figuring things out.

These people are the ones who don't just tolerate who you are but celebrate it. The ones who don't just accept your existence but actively pour into you, uplift you, and remind you of your worth when you forget it.

Chosen family is the reassuring text message on a hard day, the presence in the audience when you least expect it, the voice on the other end of the line that tells you, "You got this." It's knowing that even if the world doubts you, even if some doors close in your face, there are people who will always open theirs to you.

Some of the most profound moments of grounding in my life haven't happened in churches, at family gatherings, or in grand moments of realization. They've happened in the small moments—the ones that seem insignificant at the time but stay with you forever:

Sitting on the phone, talking for hours, feeling understood in a way words can't fully express.

Hearing, "I'm proud of you," from a friend at the exact moment I needed to hear it.

Laughing so hard my stomach hurt, reminded me that joy is just as sacred as struggle.

Being able to be silent in someone's presence, no pressure to entertain, just the comfort of knowing they are there.

The beauty of a chosen family is that these are the people who show up—not just when it's convenient, not just for the highlights, but for the in-between moments that make up real life.

One of the greatest lessons I've learned is that your chosen family is just as important as the one you were born into. Because sometimes, we need people who love us not because they have to, but because they want to. There is something deeply affirming about knowing that the people in your life have actively chosen to stay.

It's a different kind of love. A love that is free of obligation, full of intention. A love that says: I see you. I choose you. You are enough just as you are. And at the end of the day, isn't that what we all want? To be loved, not out of duty, but out of deliberate, unwavering choice?

Love is what keeps us steady. It is what makes life rich, what gives us a place to return to when the world feels like too much.
I have spent my life chasing growth, chasing success, chasing purpose. But the older I get, the more I realize that none of it matters if you don't have love.

Love is the thing that keeps you from losing yourself. It is the thing that reminds you of where you came from, no matter how far you go. And if I have learned anything, it is this: What grounds you will always be stronger than what tries to break you. Brown is home. Brown is love. Brown is the thing that keeps me steady.

Chapter 12: Gold

The Impact I Leave Behind

Gold is the color of legacy, of value, of what remains when everything else fades. It is the color of lessons passed down, of seeds planted in the lives of others, of the impact that lingers long after we are gone.

For me, gold represents the imprint of my journey—the ways I have poured into others, the lessons I have learned and shared, and the responsibility I carry to uplift those who come after me. Legacy is not just about titles, awards, or public recognition. It is about the people we touch, the lives we change, and the ways we make the world just a little bit better.

But legacy is a complicated thing. It is not just about what we choose to leave behind—it is also about what we inherit. Whether we realize it or not, each of us carries pieces of those who came before us. We inherit their wisdom, their struggles, their sacrifices. Some of those inheritances are gifts—guiding lights that help us navigate our own path. Others are burdens—expectations and unspoken rules about who we are supposed to be and how we are supposed to show up in the world.

I used to think that legacy was something reserved for the greats, for people whose names are etched into history books. But I have come to realize that legacy is not measured by fame—it is measured by impact. It is measured by the way we make people feel, the wisdom we share, the love we give, and the spaces we create for others to thrive.

And if we are not intentional about our legacy, someone else will define it for us. The world will decide what we stood for, what we represented, and what we left behind. So, I have made the conscious choice to own my legacy, to be deliberate about the mark I leave on this world.

This chapter explores the meaning of legacy in my life—the ways I have been shaped by those who came before me and how I hope to shape those who come after me. It is about the mentors, the students, the friendships, and the communities that have woven themselves into my story. It is about purpose, responsibility, and the commitment to leaving something greater than myself behind. Because at the end of the day, what we build for ourselves will fade, but what we build for others will last.

Maya Angelou once said, *"I've learned that people will forget what you said, people will forget what you did, but people will never forget how you made them feel."* That quote has resonated with me for as long as I can remember because it encapsulates what legacy truly is.

When we think about legacy, we often think of things that can be measured—titles, accomplishments, buildings named after us, books written, positions held. But when I consider what I want to leave behind, it isn't something that can be recorded on a résumé or carved into stone. It is something felt. It is the imprint I leave on hearts, the way people remember experiencing me, the way my presence made others feel valued and loved.

Life is filled with interactions—small moments that may seem insignificant at the time but live on in the memories of others long after we are gone. Every day, we have opportunities to shape how people will remember us, to plant seeds of kindness, to stand for something greater than ourselves, to embody love in a world that so often lacks it. When I reflect on my own journey, I think about the people who have made an impact on me—not just through their words, but through their unwavering presence, their encouragement, their belief in me even when I struggled to believe in myself. That is the kind of legacy I want to leave behind.

When people think of me, I want them to remember that I loved God and that I loved His people. That I treated others with dignity and respect, regardless of whether they agreed with me, looked like me, or believed the same things I did. That love, for me, was an action, not just a word. That I did not just speak about justice—I stood for it. That I did not just talk about grace—I extended it. That I did not just preach about mercy—I practiced it.

I want my life to be a reminder that love is not passive—it is active, it is intentional, it is fierce. Love means advocating for people when they cannot advocate for themselves. Love means showing up, even when it's inconvenient. Love means choosing to be kind, not because it is easy, but because it is necessary. I want my legacy to be one of action—of choosing grace over retaliation, of using my voice to uplift instead of tear down, of making the people in my life feel seen, heard, and valued.

More than anything, I want my legacy to be one of compassion, advocacy, and radical love. I want the people I have crossed paths with to remember that I fought for the things that mattered, that I used my voice to uplift those who needed it, and that I lived with intentionality. Not perfectly, not without mistakes, but with the deep conviction that my existence was meant to bring light into the world.

At the end of the day, legacy is not about being remembered by the masses. It is about being remembered by the people who mattered—those whose lives I touched, whose spirits I lifted, whose burdens I helped carry. And if, when my time here is done, people can say that I made them feel loved, valued, and seen, then I will have lived a life worth remembering.

I think about the small moments, the quiet acts of love that leave an impression long after words fade. The times I took a phone call late at night just to listen. The handwritten notes of encouragement. The times I showed up for someone, not because I had to, but because I wanted to. I think about the times someone was there for me in the same way, how their kindness changed the trajectory of my day, sometimes even my life.

That is legacy. It is not just what we build; it is how we build people. It is not just what we accomplish; it is the kindness we extend along the way. It is not just about being remembered—it is about being remembered for the right things.

I am not here by accident. I am the product of generations of love, sacrifice, and resilience. I stand on the shoulders of those who paved the way—who faced struggles I will never fully comprehend, who made choices that ensured I had more opportunities than they did, who saw a future for me that was brighter than the one they were given. Their sacrifices were not in vain. Their prayers did not go unheard. Their labor, their wisdom, their unshakable belief in me—those things live on in me.

My mother, my grandmother, my mentors—they shaped me long before I even knew I was being molded. They poured into me before I understood the weight of what they were giving. They held me up when I was learning to walk, and they held me up again when I was learning how to navigate life's complexities.

I think about my grandmother—her unwavering support, the way she never let me shrink, never let me doubt, never let the world tell me I was anything less than worthy. She made me feel like I could do anything, and because of her, I believed it. When I succeeded, she was there. When I failed, she reminded me that failure was not the end, just another lesson. In her eyes, I could do no wrong, and that unconditional love gave me the confidence to become the person I am today.

I think about my mother—her strength, her faith, and the countless sacrifices she made without ever asking for recognition. She was the quiet but steady force that kept everything together, making sure that no matter what was happening in the world outside, home was a place of love, safety, and support. She always had an answer, always had a way of making things work, even when I didn't realize how much effort it took. She pushed me to be excellent, not because she needed me to succeed for her own pride, but because she knew what I was capable of before I did. Her love was both tender and firm—a reminder that I could always come home, but that I also had the strength to stand on my own. Everything I am today is because of her prayers, her wisdom, and her unyielding belief in me.

I think about the mentors who saw something in me before I saw it in myself. The ones who encouraged me to step up, to lead, to speak, to teach. The ones who recognized my potential when I was still learning to recognize it in myself. There were moments when I doubted my ability, when I hesitated to step into spaces I felt unworthy of—but they never let me settle for playing small. They challenged me to embrace my gifts, to take up space, to understand that I belonged in every room

I walked into. They invested their time, their wisdom, and their belief in me, and that belief made all the difference.

And then there are the quiet heroes—the ones whose names history may never record, but whose impact will last for generations. The ancestors I never got to meet, but whose strength runs through my veins. The family members who worked long hours in fields, factories, and kitchens, who endured hardships so that one day, someone like me could sit in boardrooms, classrooms, and leadership positions.

Their legacy is in me. Their prayers covered me before I was even born. Their resilience set the foundation for everything I am able to do. When I speak, I carry their voices. When I move forward, I take their dreams with me. When I succeed, it is because of the sacrifices they made long before I had the language to understand them. Everything I do is an extension of their investment.

So, when I work, I do it with intention. When I speak, I do it with conviction. When I lead, I do it with humility. Because I am not just living for myself—I am continuing the story they started. And that is the greatest honor of all.

And yet, being in spaces where people like me are often absent is both a privilege and a burden. Representation matters, but it comes with responsibility. I have always been aware of the weight I carry when I step into certain rooms. The weight of being the first, the only, the one expected to pave the way for others. The weight of knowing that my success is not just about me—it is about those who will come after me, those who will look at my journey and see that it is possible for them too.

There is an unspoken pressure that comes with breaking barriers. It is the pressure to excel, to perform, to never make a mistake because your failure will not be seen as an individual failure—it will be seen as confirmation of what they already believed about people like you.

I have felt that pressure. I have carried it. But I have also learned that my presence is enough. That I do not have to prove my worth by being perfect. That I belong in every room I enter because I have earned my place, not because I am a symbol or an exception.

I carry this responsibility not as a burden, but as a privilege. Because I know that by standing in these spaces, I make room for others. And that, in itself, is legacy.

Legacy is not built on moments of recognition—it is built in the quiet, unseen ways we pour into others. It is built in the lives we touch, the students we mentor, the people we uplift.

One of the most fulfilling aspects of my life has been mentorship. Being able to guide, support, and encourage others on their journey has been one of the most meaningful parts of my work.

I have seen students walk into classrooms doubting themselves and walk out knowing they are capable. I have seen mentees step into leadership roles, knowing they are prepared because someone took the time to invest in them. These moments mean more than any award ever could.

I do not measure my success by what I have accomplished. I measure it by how many people I have helped along the way. Because that is the work that will outlive me.

As I continue this journey, I remind myself that legacy is not something I am waiting to build—it is something I am building every day. It is in the people I mentor. It is in the lives I impact. It is in the words I leave behind, in the love I give, in the ways I show up.

I do not know how history will remember me. But I do know that I will leave behind something meaningful. I know that my story, my journey, and my impact will live on—not just in what I accomplish, but in the people I uplift along the way. That is the gold I leave behind. That is my legacy.

Conclusion: Embracing Every Color of My Story

As I reach the final pages of this book, I find myself looking both backward and forward. This memoir has been a reflection of where I've been—the struggles, the victories, the lessons—but my story is far from over. Life is still unfolding, still painting itself in colors I have yet to discover.

For so long, I viewed my experiences as separate brushstrokes, moments that existed in isolation. The hardships, the triumphs, the setbacks, the revelations—they all felt like disconnected events, each carrying its own weight, each defining its own chapter. But now, I see them for what they truly are—parts of a greater masterpiece, a story still being written. A canvas that is still evolving.

Each chapter has carried its own shade, its own emotions, its own defining moments. There have been times of brilliance and times of darkness. There have been seasons where I felt unstoppable, where I walked in my purpose with unwavering confidence. And there have been seasons where I questioned everything, where doubt clouded my vision, where I wondered if I was on the right path at all. But through it all, I have come to understand that every color, every experience, has a place.

I have carried wounds, and I have carried wisdom. I have fought to prove myself, and I have learned to simply be. I have loved, I have lost, and I have found myself in the in-between. But most importantly—I have grown. And I am still growing.

Because that is what life is—a continuous evolution, an ever-expanding palette of experiences that shape us, challenge us, and mold us into the people we are becoming. There is no final version of me. No endpoint. No destination where I suddenly have it all figured out. There is only the journey. And that journey is still unfolding in front of me.

If there's anything I've learned, it's that transformation is not a one-time event. It is not a moment of awakening that happens once and never again. It is a continual process, an unfolding, an evolution.

There was a time when I believed that healing meant reaching a final destination, that growth had a finish line. But the truth is, there is no final version of me. There is no version of myself that will have it all figured out, no point where I stop learning, stop feeling, stop changing. And that is a beautiful thing.

Because it means I still have life to live. I still have dreams to chase. I still have love to give. I still have a future that is waiting for me, full of possibilities I have yet to imagine.

There is no roadmap for what comes next, no perfect formula for how to move forward. But what I do know is this: I am walking into my future without fear.

While the past has shaped me, it does not define my future. The best part of my story has yet to be written. Every experience, every lesson, and every challenge has prepared me for what's next. But the beauty of life is that there is always more—more to learn, more to create, more to become.

There are still places I have yet to go, places that will stretch me, challenge me, and remind me of how much of the world I have yet to experience. There are people I have yet to meet, souls who will inspire me, encourage me, and teach me lessons I didn't even know I needed. There are lessons I have yet to learn, truths that will refine me, wisdom that will deepen my understanding of myself and the world.

There are dreams I have yet to bring to life, goals that have not yet been spoken, visions that are still taking shape, ideas that will push me beyond my comfort zone.

This memoir may be complete, but my story continues. The road ahead is still being paved, the canvas still waiting for more color. There are still blank pages waiting to be filled, still chapters that have not yet been written. There will be more growth, more discovery, more lessons. There will be moments that push me beyond my comfort zone, moments that stretch me, moments that remind me that I am still evolving. And I welcome them all.

I used to believe that life was about finding certainty, about reaching a place where everything made sense. But now, I see that life is about embracing the unknown, about being open to the unexpected, about trusting that what's ahead of me is just as important as what's behind me. I am not done yet.

I will continue stepping into new spaces, challenging myself to grow beyond what I once thought was possible. I will continue creating, pouring my heart into the work that matters most to me. I will continue speaking, teaching, mentoring, writing, and finding ways to share my journey so that it might help someone else along theirs.

I will continue pushing myself toward the unknown, embracing the adventure of what's next, trusting that every step forward is leading me to exactly where I need to be. Because what's ahead of me is just as important as what's behind me. And so is what's ahead of you.

I wrote this book to remind you that your past does not limit your future. Your story is not over, and every moment—every triumph, every heartbreak, every moment of doubt—has shaped you into the person you are becoming. No part of your journey has been wasted. Even the painful moments, the missteps, and the struggles have contributed to your growth.

Whatever you have been through, whatever you have survived—it is not the end of your story. You may have walked through seasons of uncertainty, feeling like the weight of the world was too heavy to carry. You may have believed that your mistakes defined you, that your setbacks disqualified you, that the doors closed before you meant the journey was over. But hear me when I say this: You are still here. And as long as you are still here, your purpose remains.

You are still growing, even when it feels like progress is invisible. Growth isn't always loud and obvious; sometimes, it's happening quietly beneath the surface, in the way you keep showing up, in the way you refuse to give up on yourself. You are still becoming, even if you don't have all the answers yet. Your journey is not about perfection—it's about persistence. And if this book has done anything, I hope it has reminded you of this:

You are worthy of a future that excites you. You do not have to settle for a life that drains you. You have the right to dream boldly and to chase after the life you deserve.

You are deserving of love, joy, and abundance. Your worth is not based on what you achieve, what you produce, or what others think of you. You are enough, just as you are.

You are capable of turning every experience into something meaningful. Even the painful moments, even the disappointments, even the things that once broke you—they are not the end of your story. They are part of your resilience, part of your testimony, part of the masterpiece that is still being created.

So, dream. So, step forward. So, embrace what's next. Your story still matters. You still have something to give to this world. Go forward with the courage to color outside the lines, to reclaim your story, one shade at a time. And know—there is still so much more to create.

Acknowledgments

To God

First and foremost, to God, who has guided my steps even when I didn't always understand the path before me. Thank You for Your grace, Your wisdom, and the purpose You have placed within me. Every moment of doubt, every obstacle, and every triumph was part of a divine plan greater than I could have imagined. This book, and the journey it represents, would not have been possible without Your unwavering presence in my life. Thank You for being my strength when I had none, my light when the way felt unclear, and my reminder that my purpose is far greater than my pain.

To My Ancestors

To my ancestors, whose prayers, sacrifices, and resilience are embedded in my very existence—this book is a tribute to you. You carried burdens I will never fully know, yet you walked forward with dignity, faith, and the unshakable determination to create something better for those who came after you. I honor you, not just in words, but in action. Your stories live on in me, and I strive to continue the work you began. Thank you for the strength in my bones, the wisdom in my spirit, and the fire in my soul.

To My Family

To my family, the ones who poured into me even when I didn't always recognize the value of what you were giving—thank you. Your love, your lessons, and your belief in me shaped the person I have become. You have been my foundation, my safe space, and my greatest teachers. To my parents, who instilled in me the importance of education, resilience, and faith—your sacrifices did not go unnoticed.

To my brother, thank you for reminding me where I come from and pushing me to be the best version of myself. I am forever grateful for the ways you have colored my world with love, laughter, and lessons that I carry with me every day.

To My Friends

To my friends, the ones who have stood by me in every season—thank you for your unwavering support, your laughter, your late-night conversations, and your ability to remind me of who I am when I sometimes forget. Your encouragement has been a lifeline. You have celebrated my wins, carried me through my struggles, and challenged me to keep growing. Friendship is a rare and precious gift, and I am blessed beyond measure to have each of you in my life.

To My Alpha Phi Alpha Fraternity Brothers

To my brothers of Alpha Phi Alpha Fraternity, Inc., the men who have uplifted, challenged, and inspired me—you are an integral part of my journey. Our bond is built on a commitment to manly deeds, scholarship, and love for all mankind, and I am proud to stand among you. Through the years, you have shown me the true meaning of brotherhood—not just in words, but in action. Your guidance, accountability, and encouragement have been invaluable, and I carry our shared mission with me in all that I do. Thank you for your support and for always pushing me to walk in excellence.

To My Mentors & Educators

To the mentors and educators who truly saw me—not just as a student, but as a person with something valuable to offer the world—thank you for your wisdom, your patience, and your willingness to invest in my potential. Your words, guidance, and belief in me have left a lasting imprint on my life. And to those who overlooked me, dismissed me, or failed to recognize my worth—thank you as well. You taught me the power of perseverance, the necessity of self-advocacy, and the importance of proving to myself what I already knew to be true: that I was more than capable, more than enough.

To My Students—Past, Present, and Future

To my students—past, present, and future—you are the reason I continue to do this work. You have challenged me, inspired me, and pushed me to grow just as much as I have tried to do for you. Teaching is not just about delivering knowledge; it's about cultivating curiosity, nurturing confidence, and creating spaces where all voices are heard.

To my past students, thank you for allowing me to be part of your journey. Watching you evolve, take ownership of your dreams, and step into your greatness has been one of my greatest honors.

To my present students, I hope you find in me a mentor, a supporter, and a believer in your potential. Your journey is just beginning, and I am grateful to witness the brilliance that you are becoming.

To my future students, I have yet to meet you, but I already believe in you. I hope this book serves as a reminder that your voice matters, your dreams are valid, and your presence in this world is necessary. Never let anyone define your potential—your story is yours to write, and your colors are yours to create.

To My Book Focus Group

To my Book Focus Group, the incredible individuals who took the time to engage with these pages before they were finalized—thank you. Your thoughtful feedback, honest reflections, and encouragement meant more than I can express. Writing can be a solitary process, but you reminded me that this story was never just about me—it was about all of us. I am deeply grateful for your time, your perspective, and your belief in this work.

To Those Who See Themselves in This Story

To every child who has ever felt unseen. To every student who was told to quiet their voice. To every individual who has been made to believe they don't belong—you are proof that we are meant to color beyond the lines. You were never too much. You were never not enough. You were always meant to take up space.

This book is not just my story—it is a reflection of the people and experiences that have shaped me. It is a testament to resilience, to growth, and to the power of reclaiming our narratives. And for that, I am forever grateful.

—Dr. B.T. McGuire

DR. B.T. MCGUIRE

Dr. B.T. McGuire is an educational developer, professor, and author dedicated to personal growth, leadership, and transformation. As the author of *Whispers of Wisdom: Navigating 30 Life Epiphanies for Transformation* and *The Effective Educator: Research-Based Strategies for Classroom Success*, he empowers individuals to embrace their journeys and redefine success on their own terms.

A 2022 Black Nashville Top Forty Under 40 honoree, his work bridges education, mentorship, and storytelling, making him a sought-after voice in personal and professional development.

Connect with Dr. B.T. McGuire: [www.drbtmcguire.com]

www.ingramcontent.com/pod-product-compliance
Lightning Source LLC
Chambersburg PA
CBHW050519100526
44581CB00001B/37